2004

Dear Camille,

I hope these beautiful words bring you peace and comfort.

Love,
Terry

Praise for *A Tempered Faith*

from America's Spiritual and Political Leaders

A love story for the ages. I couldn't put it down. This book will make you cry and laugh as it teaches you the meaning of a true faith in God and reveals Christianity's gigantic secret: the power of joy.

—*Fr. John Catoir, President, St. Jude Media Ministry, author of* The Joy Trilogy

Jennifer's inspiring personal journey through numbing tragedy to God's loving embrace is a compelling testimony to the supernatural healing found in Christ.

—*Congressman Christopher H. Smith (R-NJ), Chairman, U.S. Helsinki Commission*

Loss is always difficult—and to lose one we love dearly so unexpectedly, tragically, rocks our boat until we are sure that the waves will surely sink us. Jennifer Sands has shared her discovery of how to calm the winds. "Peace—be still," is the voice that resounds through our souls even amid today's troubled waters. There is so much we can learn about weathering life's storms in the pages of this book. God bless you, Jennifer, for having the courage to open your heart, that others might find the strength and courage to journey on through faith in and commitment to the One who truly understands all pain and loss.

—*Janette Oke, author of* Love Comes Softly

Jennifer Sands not only writes the impressive personal story of her continuing post-9/11 journey through disbelief, suicidal despair and bitter anger with God. Perhaps more, she offers a precious gift of encouragement and strength to those like her who grieve a loved one, and who are searching how to say goodbye with hope.

—*Fr. John Dietzen, author,* Catholic Life in the New Century, *syndicated columnist,* Catholic News Service

A Tempered Faith is the love story of Jennifer and Jim Sands, but it's also the story of a spiritual rebirth that has enabled Jennifer to deal with the loss of her young husband on 9/11/01. Jennifer recounts her extraordinary tale of rebellion against God, her return to Him, and her ultimate ability to focus on Jim's life, not his death. Her journey of faith inspires us all to remember that the 9/11 victims live on within us and must never be forgotten.

—*Senator Andrew R. Ciesla, New Jersey State Senate*

Much has been said and written about the tragic events of September 11, 2001—a day that changed our nation and forced people not only in the United States, but throughout the world to recognize the reality of hatred and evil. While this global story is very real, underlying it are the lives of ordinary people—people who would wake each morning, head off to work, celebrate the gift of love, make a home, and share dreams and hopes for the future.

Jennifer Sands shares with us the story of her life's hopes together with her husband Jim who died in the attack on the World Trade Center in New York on 9/11. This is a powerful story of faith in the midst of grieving, and it reveals that trust in God is indeed a powerful grace, empowering us to rise above feelings of hopelessness and continue to dream.

—*Most Rev. John M. Smith Bishop of Trenton*

A Tempered Faith

Rediscovering Hope
in the Ashes of Loss

A Tempered Faith

Rediscovering Hope in the Ashes of Loss

Jennifer Sands

With a Foreword by New Jersey Governor James E. McGreevey

A Surviving Spirit in the Wake of the World Trade Center Tragedy

The Olive Press, an imprint of Peak Writing, LLC,
37 W. Fairmont Ave., Suite 202, Savannah, Ga. 31406

Feedback to the author: jennifer@jennifersands.com

For information regarding special discounts for bulk purchases, please contact Buhrmaster Marketing at 1-773-481-4964 or specialsales@theolivepress.net.

Cover and interior design by Pneuma Books, LLC
For more information, visit www.pneumabooks.com

Publisher's Cataloging-in-Publication
(Provided by Quality Books, Inc.)

Sands, Jennifer
    A tempered faith : rediscovering hope in the ashes of
loss / by Jennifer Sands. -- 1st ed.
    p. cm.
    LCCN 2003106020
    ISBN 0971733074

    1. Sands, Jennifer. 2. Sands, Jim. 3. Christian
biography. 4. September 11 Terrorist Attacks, 2001.
5. Victims of terrorism--New Jersey--Brick (Township)--
Biography. 6. Terrorism victims' families--New Jersey--
Brick (Township)--Biography.   I. Title.

BR1725.S2687A3 2003   277.3'083092
                        QBI33-1384

09 08 07 06 05 04 03   6 5 4 3 2 1

For Jim…

I, Jennifer, take you, Jim, to be my husband…
I promise to love you, honor you, cherish you, respect you,
and adore you…

All the days of my life.

Can't wait to see you again, hon.

Contents

1   Burnt Popcorn   1

2   It Had to Be You   7

3   Oh My God, Jen, Is Jim Okay?   13

4   Brain Lock   19

5   Another Xanax Day   25

6   What Dreams May Come   29

7   The Black Hole   33

8   God, How Dare You?   39

9   Angels from Above   45

10   Something to Look forward To   53

11   Reality Bricks   59

12   The Husband Card   65

13   The Rose and the Lenox Vase   69

14   WTCW and KITA   75

15   Constant Reminders, Constant Gratitude   81

16   Getting around on Crutches   89

17   Jim Sands Memorial Reef   93

18   The Two-Headed Guilt Monster   103

19   Condolences: Round Two   109

20   Witness for the Defense   117

21   The First Christmas   121

22   September 11, 2002   125

23   Crying with Hope   131

24   A 9/11 Diary   135

Photographs

Jim & Jennifer. Christmas, 1997 *x*
"Grieving Angel" sculpture 82
Jim Sands Memorial Reef plaque 94
Jim Sands "Missing" Poster 181

A Word from the Governor of New Jersey

As a nation, the events of September 11th shattered our domestic tranquility and threatened us all. Our neighbors died; our buildings fell. The images will forever be etched in our minds.

The attacks also left a deep and lasting emotional impact. It is this human side of September 11th and its aftermath that Jennifer Sands captures in *A Tempered Faith: Rediscovering Hope in the Ashes of Loss.*

The book is interspersed with vignettes about Jennifer's life with her husband Jim, who worked in the World Trade Center as a strategic development engineer for Cantor Fitzgerald. We learn about their wedding, we hear their conversations as movie buffs and football fans, and we share their dreams of retiring in the Cayman Islands.

Jennifer takes us into a world that only those who have lost loved ones suddenly and tragically have experienced — shopping for greeting cards and realizing she'll never buy her husband a card again, appointment reminders that continue to be seen on Jim's laptop computer, realizing the CD that came on when she started his car was the last song he heard, and finding a Christmas gift he had bought her and hidden in their attic.

We get to know Jim and Jennifer Sands as people — not just

as statistics or as the KITA (Killed in Terrorist Attack) and WTCW (World Trade Center Widow) references which now identify them on legal documents.

As Governor of the State of New Jersey, it has been a privilege for me to work with Jennifer and the other families in the aftermath of September 11th. They are people of tremendous courage and dignity. And as Jennifer acknowledges in her book, the incredible outpouring of support from our state and our nation has been an inspiration and a reaffirmation of the American spirit which the terrorists attempted to break.

Rather than break our spirit, the attacks have made us more determined and more resolved.

A few days after September 11th, I had the opportunity to witness firsthand the site of the tragedy and the gruesome search throughout the World Trade Center graveyard that yielded no survivors. I was in awe of the many exhausted emergency workers of every kind — police, firemen and volunteers who acted as though there was nothing special to what they were doing. For them, they were acting out of a sense of duty. They walked forward until they found something that needed doing and then they did it.

Clearly, we are at our best as a people, as a state and as a nation when we help one another — and government is at its best when it is guided by strong leadership in partnership with the people. On the first anniversary of the attacks, I suggested that we vow to honor those who died by rising above the evil that claimed their lives and that we eulogize them with our strength.

In *A Tempered Faith*, Jennifer Sands has done just that.

James E. McGreevey, Governor
State of New Jersey

Grasped by the Power of God's Promise

Holding this book, you are not just reading a story, you are experiencing a life. In her pit of blackness, plunged there by sudden, incomprehensible tragedy, Jennifer Sands met a new person — herself. She had become someone she couldn't possibly know — altered, chopped, bleeding, screaming, but ultimately reshaped enough to glimpse light again. Jennifer tells her experience with utter and profound honesty, as anyone who has been plunged into that same pit of darkness — losing a loved one because of a violent, evil act — can well verify. I know, because I, too, like Jennifer, had to admit my confused, distorted, altered self, my anger at God and the world, and my desperate need to find hope when my son and daughter-in-law were murdered by an eighteen-year old with a gun in his hand.

In reading Jennifer's gut-honest recounting of her ultimate determination to live and to bring her hurt to God, humbly trusting in His will to heal her, I relived my own difficult journey. Like Jennifer, who I relate to now as a "sister" from the sharing of her story in this powerful book, I sought enlightenment from spiritual guides, and as she did, I found a new understanding of faith. The wisdom words of Paul Tillich touched me: "Faith means being grasped by a power that is greater than we are, a power that shakes us and turns us and transforms us and heals us." I believe that's the faith Jennifer expresses in this book, a level of faith so hard to reach, but so regenerating when we begin to believe we can get there.

Great attention has been given to the tragic events of September 11th, including much talk of compensation, heroes, rebuilding the site with proper memorials, and more. But I have read nothing which so grabbed my attention or touched my heart as Jennifer's story. For when the final dust has settled about the destruction of that day, and the historians have rightly recorded it for posterity, what must not be forgotten was that once again man's inhumanity to man brought horrendous destruction into the lives of individuals and families.

Yet, God's grace becomes the healing force for some, like Jennifer. In telling her story, she has given us a permanent gift — renewed hope — that, although we may not understand God's apparent absence in a world where evil often thrives, we are not alone. She learned, as I have, that while God doesn't give us answers, or end our pain, God gives us a promise: "I am always with you." And that assurance, in the end, is enough.

Antoinette Bosco is a syndicated columnist for the Catholic News Service and author of the bestselling The Pummeled Heart: Finding Peace through Pain *and* Shaken Faith: Hanging in There When God Seems Far Away.

See, I have refined you, though not as silver; I have tested you in the furnace of affliction.

~Isaiah 48: 10 (NIV)

Two A.M. We're asleep. Jim rolls over – too close to the edge – tumbles out of the bed and lands on the floor with a thud.

I bolt up. "What happened? You okay?" I can barely see him in the darkness.

"Bad dismount," Jim mumbles. "That's why you gotta stick the landing. It's the last thing the judges see."

Burnt Popcorn

1

It's the evening of September 10, 2001, and the New York Giants are going to be on Monday Night Football in a few hours. This is a very big deal for us: Jim and I are huge Giants fans. They play home games at New Jersey's Meadowlands, only an hour from our house, and they're our team. Okay, they stink this year. We know this and accept it, yet we're loyal to the end.

I'm stuck at work until 9:00 P.M. and can't wait to get home, snuggle up on the couch with my honey, and scream at Kerry Collins for throwing yet another interception. Jim has promised to cook our favorite pasta — Gemelli.

Dinner is a disaster. I'm Italian, so jarred sauce is a sacrilege, yet we're forced to use it some nights, especially when I work late at the pharmacy. Jim has chosen a new Burgundy wine concoction. We both take one bite and Jim declares, "Well, we won't be repeating this one."

Close to midnight and still only in the third quarter, the Giants are getting stomped. Jim decides to make his signature popcorn — melting his own butter, grinding his own sea salt — as a replacement dinner, even though he has to get up in only five hours to go to work. Like I said, a true, die-hard fan.

Jim burns the popcorn. I smell the charred mess as soon as

he sits down with the big bowl in his lap. He knows I hate it when he burns the popcorn.

"How can you stand eating that?" I ask him.

He shrugs his shoulders. "I don't mind," he says and proceeds to devour the entire bowl by himself.

We stay up until 1:00 A.M. Of course the Giants lose the game, and of course we lose precious sleep.

At 4:00 A.M. I'm awakened by the sound of Jim fumbling through his nightstand for a bottle of pills. As a pharmacist I'm acutely aware of the sound that pills make in a bottle. I can identify a pill based solely on the sound it makes when rattled. Jim's bottle is making a sound I know all too well : Pepto-Bismol tablets.

"Are you okay?" I ask.

He replies with a series of grunts and moans that can be loosely interpreted as, "Uuuggghhhhh, my stomach."

"Serves you right for eating that burnt popcorn."

"Uuuggghhhhh."

An hour later, the alarm goes off and Jim climbs out of bed to begin his routine: a shower and ten cups of coffee from his "coffee stein," which is five times larger than any known mug. I begin my own routine of dozing on and off, making sure he stays on schedule and waiting for him to kiss me goodbye promptly at 5:50 A.M. I'm wondering how he can function at all after staying up to that ungodly hour and getting sick to boot. I'm glad Tuesdays are my day off so I can sleep a little later to make up for last night.

At 6:05 A.M. I'm still half awake when I hear his footsteps next to the bed.

"Bye, hon," Jim says, leaning over me.

I feel his lips on mine. I see the familiar angles of his face in the dark room backlit from the hallway. Then I smell him — my Jim.

"You're late," I say. My hand finds the back of his head then moves to his cheek, fresh and smooth from the razor.

"Yup. I'm late."

"Hmmph. I wonder why."

"Rahrahrahrahrah." This is Jim's comic imitation of me nagging him.

"I love you," I murmur.

"I love *you*."

I notice that he says it differently than normal. He accents the "you" and leaves off the "too." His words are clear, articulate, and purposeful — unlike his usually slurred, early morning "Luvyatoo." I wonder, as I lie there watching his dark form move toward the light, why he sounds so ... happy.

"Call me later," I remind him, even though he always calls or e-mails me from work, usually around 10:00 A.M.

"Okay," he says. And then he is gone.

Now for the last step of my routine. Must pray for his safety. Must stay awake long enough to pray. Can't fall back to sleep yet. It's Murphy's Law. The one time I don't pray for him, that's when something will happen.

So I whisper the same little prayer that I say every morning as he leaves for work: *Please, God, get him to work safely, and bring him home safely, too. He's everything in the world to me, and I love him so much. So please, Lord, watch over him.*

I hate that commute. Jim hates it even more. He drives forty-five minutes to Atlantic Highlands to catch a commuter ferry for another forty-five-minute ride up the Hudson River. Then comes a ten-minute walk through Lower Manhattan to Tower One of the World Trade Center followed by a fifteen-minute elevator ride to the 103rd floor after changing elevators at the 78th floor. I'm always so afraid of car accidents, ferries capsizing, dangerous criminals lurking the city streets. Worry, worry, worry. I worry about everything. Almost everything. Surely praying to God will protect Jim from all that. Prayer is powerful. God is almighty. I have faith.

I hear the garage door close and fall back to sleep.

Jim's favorite routine when asked about our relationship:

"I'm the luckiest guy I know. I married my spirit's twin and my soul's mirror." (Pause)

"Hey, wait a minute! I married an obsessive, compulsive Sicilian. Was I delusional?" (Wink)

It Had
to Be You

2

Jim and I have always loved the song *It Had to Be You*. We liked Harry Connick's rendition, but we especially enjoyed the version sung by Marla Hooch in the movie *A League of Their Own* as she croons (like nails on a chalkboard) to her future husband.

I met my future husband through a dating service. We bought each other. I got Jim on sale — they were running a special. Biggest bargain of my life, that's for sure. But we both could have saved time and a few thousand dollars if we had just walked down the street and waved hello to each other. How's this for irony...

I was born Jennifer Ann Trebino on April 2, 1964, the youngest of three children. I grew up in a quiet neighborhood called Point Pleasant Manor in the small (at the time) town of Brick, New Jersey. I was born and raised there, graduating from Brick Memorial High School in 1982. I then moved to Philadelphia for five years to attend Philadelphia College of Pharmacy and Science. After earning my pharmacy degree and getting my license, I moved back to the old neighborhood and eventually bought a house just five blocks away from where I grew up. I began working for a busy, independent pharmacy (I'm still there) just a few minutes from my home. After several failed relationships, years of fruitless searches for my soul mate and life partner, and downright desperation, I joined the Together dating service in January 1995.

Jim was born James Sands Jr., on May 24, 1963, the youngest of three children. He grew up in a quiet neighborhood called Point Pleasant Manor in the small (at the time) town of Brick, New Jersey. He was born and raised there, graduating from Brick High School in 1981 (sound familiar yet?) and Monmouth University in 1985 with a bachelor's degree in biology. He then moved to New York for five years in pursuit of a career in computer engineering. In 1990 he moved back to the old neighborhood and bought a house just seven blocks away from the home he grew up in. He began working as a software engineer from his home office for a New York-based company called Marketvision. After several failed relationships, years of fruitless searches for his soul mate and life partner, and downright desperation, he joined the Together dating service in December 1994, one month before I did.

The punch line: We never knew each other until the service set us up. We lived only blocks away from each other our entire lives. Jim was one year older than I, and we attended the same schools (except for the last two years of high school, when the town built a new school and split up the classes.) We rode the same school bus. We knew each other's friends, yet we did not know each other. We each purchased our own homes in the same development that we grew up in, yet we still never met. Our paths must have crossed hundreds of times over thirty-one years. But it took an expensive dating service for us to finally bump into each other. Go figure.

Our first (and blind) date was on May 27, 1995. After getting over the shock and confusion of how we could have possibly *not* known each other — "You grew up where? So did I!" "You now

8

live where? So do I!" — we both realized there was something very special happening. It was truly "love at first sight," and the years of fruitless searches were over. We had finally found our soul mates. We were engaged less than three months later and married on May 4, 1996 — less than one year after we met.

From that first date until the day he died, Jim and I were inseparable. We had so much in common: same dreams, same goals, same likes and dislikes. We met every one of the criteria on the "Wish List" we each submitted to the dating service: We came from similar upbringings. We enjoyed many of the same hobbies and sports. We were both non-smokers and non-drinkers. Both over-achievers.

We had something that few people are ever fortunate to have: a fairytale marriage. Before our wedding day, we secretly trained with a professional dance instructor for seven months so that our first dance would be a grand Viennese waltz performed to music from Tchaikovsky's *Swan Lake*. The crowd oohed and ahhed.

We never fought. No, I'm not sentimentalizing. We honestly never had a fight. We rarely disagreed, and if we did, there was always a compromise — usually Jim's. It was like we were the same person — just male and female versions of each other. We shared a strong love and an unbreakable bond.

After my big, fat, Catholic wedding, I continued to work full-time at the pharmacy, and Jim eventually left Marketvision (and the comfort of working from home) for a ninety-minute commute to Optimark, a computer software company where he worked as a strategic development engineer for the financial markets. Jim led the team that developed the software used in stock trading systems for NASDAQ and other stock markets, and he soon became a leading engineer in the computer industry. Recall that Jim's education consisted of a biology (not an engineering) degree. Everything he learned about computers he taught himself from books or learned by example, and now he was playing with the big boys from MIT and Columbia. Yet he was highly respected, admired, and well liked by his peers.

But in December 2000 Optimark fell into financial trouble, and Jim's job stability was threatened. He had several offers and opportunities with other companies, but he decided to jump on board with eSpeed, a division of Cantor Fitzgerald, the largest bond brokerage firm in the world. The only drawback was the two-hour commute from our home in New Jersey to the 103rd floor of the World Trade Center in New York. We thought the new salary, which was far higher than he had ever previously earned, would more than compensate for the commute. So in January 2001, Jim began working for eSpeed as a strategic development engineer, writing software to be used in trading systems for the government bond market.

Our goal at this time was to save enough money to purchase property in Grand Cayman, British West Indies. We both shared a strong passion for scuba diving, and our dream was to eventually retire from our fast-paced careers and begin a new life as dive instructors in the Caribbean. We planned to buy a small condo on Grand Cayman to rent out until we could retire and live there ourselves. We called this the five-year plan, based on our calculations of how long it would realistically take to purchase property on the island. During our last trip to Cayman for our fifth wedding anniversary in May 2001, we began to seriously research the island's real estate.

The commute to New York began to take its toll on Jim. He

10

had to leave the house by 5:50 A.M. in order to beat commuter traffic. He usually didn't get home until 8:00 P.M., exhausted from work and four hours of traveling each day. But we were also committed to our five-year plan. I kept thinking, *Hang in there, hon. You can do it!*

tf

We're going through the benefits package from Jim's new job at eSpeed to pick out insurance options.

"This life insurance section reads like Chinese stereo instructions. And the rates are astronomical," Jim says. "I should shop around for a cheaper policy."

"Uh huh." *I'm concentrating on health insurance.*

"Hon, listen. This is important. We have to have good life insurance now. I'm working in a place that's a prime target for terrorism."

I stare at him in astonishment, then burst out laughing. "Yeah, right, I'm sure. Hon, if anything is going to happen, it's going to be when you're diving. You know, high risk sport and all."

Jim is surprised I'm not taking him seriously. "It happened once," *he says.* "You think it can't happen again?"

Oh My God, Jen, Is Jim Okay?

3

It's a few minutes before 9:00 A.M. My gym bag is packed, and I'm ready for a good workout. But first I must call the pharmacy to check in and make sure I didn't leave anything pending from the night before. Maryann, a cashier, answers the phone.

"Hi. Mare. It's Jennifer. How're you do — "

She literally screams into the phone, "Oh my God, Jen, are you okay? Is Jim okay?"

"Uhhh, yeah. Why? What's going on?"

Rich, my boss and one of our dearest friends, takes the phone from Maryann.

"Jen, what floor does Jim work on?" he asks.

"The 103rd, why? What's — "

"Jen, a plane just hit the World Trade Center."

Those are some of the last words I remember from that day. I feel myself go weak, my heart pounds, I'm sick to my stomach, I'm trembling, and I can't speak. I turn on the TV in our bedroom and there it is: the most horrible sight I've ever seen.

Rich says he's on his way over to my house. I don't remember hanging up the phone, but I must have, because the phone rings. It's my mother. She's on her way over. It rings again. This time it's Jim's brother-in-law, Johnny. He and Cindy are on their way over.

Then Jim's mother. Everyone's coming. But I can't move from the TV. All I see is a burning tower. It's Tower One. Jim's tower. The one with the antenna on the top.

Oh my God. This can't be happening. Think, think. Do something. Call him!

Here's where a psychiatrist would have a field day. I'm looking at a burning skyscraper with a gaping, flaming hole right about where Jim's office window is, and suddenly I'm thinking to myself, *Wow, can't wait to hear about this one. I bet he's got a great story to tell! I can't wait till he gets home and gives us all the details!* Jim's such an entertaining storyteller. He could make an Oscar-winning story out of hanging wallpaper. This one will be amazing.

Obviously, I'm now in complete and total denial. After all, I prayed to God that morning. So nothing bad can possibly happen to Jim. Of course he'll find a way out of that building. He has to. The movie of my life always has a happy ending.

So I call Jim's office and get his voice mail. I try his cell — no answer. I call a different office number. Voice mail again. I don't bother leaving messages — I'm too desperate to find him. He must be with Paul, his good friend and office mate. They're probably whining and complaining about how they have to walk down 103 flights of stairs since the elevators are surely not working. Jim will call me. I'm sure he will.

So why isn't he calling me?

He knows how frantic I must be. He knows he's married to a panic button. The stupid phone keeps ringing, and it's everyone except Jim. I have call waiting, and I'm being rude to every well-intended person who calls: "No, I haven't heard anything, and I can't talk to you!" *Click.* Every time the phone rings, which is literally every few minutes, I say, "Please, God, let that be him." But it isn't.

Why isn't he calling me?

By now, my house is full of people. Both sides of the family, plus a few friends. Everyone is watching the nightmare unfold on Jim's new big screen TV. What a paradox. He said he wanted a television that he could view from virtually any room on the first floor, so we bought one just a few months before. And the only thing worse than watching this disaster unfold is watching it on a 60-inch screen. It amplifies the horror, complete with Dolby Surround Sound. I make every attempt not to look at it.

The second plane hits the second tower, and everyone in the room gasps collectively.

This is no accident. We're under attack.

The third plane hits the Pentagon.

This isn't happening!

The second tower collapses.

No, no…no, God, no!

I'm frantically calling Jim's office and cell phone every few minutes. But reality is starting to sink in, and so are Jim's words — his complaint about how long it takes to get from the ground floor to the 103rd floor every morning: 15 minutes in an elevator.

But now there's no elevator…

But I prayed for his safety this morning!

But it will take an hour for him to climb down 103 flights of stairs. And there's so much smoke. And he has respiratory problems…

But I prayed!

But that plane hit so close to his floor…

But God surely wouldn't let this happen!

I'm in the kitchen by myself, frantically pacing back and forth as I hit the redial button over and over. I can't stop staring at Jim's Krups coffeemaker and his empty mug in the sink. The crowd standing in front of the TV screams in unison — a spine-chilling, horrifying sound, "Oh, God! Noooooooo!"

Their voices fade into icy silence.

"What is it?" I ask.

No one answers me. They're blocking my view of the TV and someone turns the volume down.

"What happened?" I demand.

They can't even bring themselves to look at me. They're keeping their backs to me.

I scream at the top of my lungs, "WHAT HAPPENED? SOMEBODY TELL ME WHAT'S GOING ON!"

I don't recall who said it. It doesn't matter. All I hear are the words, and I know it's all over: "His tower collapsed," someone says.

And so did I.

Sitting on the bottom step of my staircase, I'm sobbing uncontrollably. I've just heard that my Uncle Frank, a pilot, was killed when his plane crashed on takeoff in Oregon. The two passengers, his wife Angie and his best friend Dan, were also killed.

Sitting next to me is this guy I just met a few days ago, Jim Sands. I hardly know him, yet I trust him completely and I don't know why. He puts his arm around me. It feels good and right and I don't want him to let go, not ever.

"I know how much this is hurting you, Jennifer. But please remember something... First of all, your Uncle Frank died quickly and painlessly. And, he died with his wife and his best friend — two people he loved dearly. If you had a choice of how you die, what more could anyone ask for?"

Brain
Lock

4

The remainder of that day is still hazy in my memory, buried deep in my subconscious, although I do recall some details. I remember sitting for long periods of time on the staircase, cleverly positioning myself so that I could not see the television and burying my head in my lap, sobbing. Then I would get up and wander around the house aimlessly in shock and disbelief, and it felt like slow motion or swimming against a current. Then suddenly I would go into screaming fits of rage. I spent a lot of time in the bathroom vomiting. I couldn't seem to become part of the efforts to find him. My brain locked up. I remember Maria, my sister, trying to console me. She came over to sit by me on the staircase.

"Let's not give up hope yet!" She put her arm around me. "You just don't know — he may have already gotten out of the building, and maybe he can't call you because they lost all phone service in the city, and — "

I cut her off. "Don't you dare give me false hope, Maria. I have to be prepared for the worst. There's no way he got out of that building in time and you know it."

Even as I said it, a part of me still expected Jim to come walking through the door, surprising us all: *Hey everybody, I'm home! Can you BELIEVE this crap?*

I jumped every time the phone rang or a door opened. People were coming and going, phones were ringing, and I was virtually dysfunctional. It was like being in an automated car wash: You're moving, but not of your own power. Chaos is happening all around you, but you're inside a bubble watching things happen, not really a part of them. Most of all, I felt completely helpless — no brake, no accelerator, no steering wheel. There was nothing I could do to stop it.

Both sides of the family began calling every hospital in Manhattan, hoping to discover that a Jim Sands had been admitted. Hours passed — still no phone call from or about Jim. Everyone was desperately trying to get information about Cantor Fitzgerald employees, but it wasn't until early evening before a hotline was set up for families to call, which gave us no more information than we already had.

I remember going into Jim's home office to check his computer for e-mail. His inbox was jam packed with frantic friends and colleagues anxious to hear from him. Desperate one-liners in the subject field like, "Are you okay???" and "Please respond soon!" and even "Cayman is worried." I replied to a few with "I haven't heard anything from Jim, and I am frantic. If you know anything at all about Cantor employees, please call me."

We kept in touch with Paul's wife, Kim. She also never got a phone call from Paul, who shared an office with Jim. Like me, she was in a state of shock and had no information on Paul's or Jim's whereabouts. The only thing we both knew was that wherever Jim and Paul were, they were together.

Close to midnight, everyone wanted me to "get some rest." But I couldn't go into our bedroom, much less lie in our bed. We had just been sleeping there, hours before, and everything was fine. It was the last place we were together, and it was too painful a reminder that everything was not fine, not anymore. It would be months before I could sleep in our bed again. The sofa in our family room became my nocturnal companion, and I was about to begin the first of many long, sleepless nights. I did lay down, crying with disbelief, my mind still not fully accepting what I knew to be the truth. Part of me was still holding on to hope of his survival, but deep down I knew. I knew.

The next morning, my sister, Maria, her husband, Tom, and Jim's sister, Loree, took the dreaded journey to Manhattan. The same images that America was watching on TV, they saw live. When they returned, their faces were masks of sadness and disbelief. The destruction they saw that day will forever haunt them. Only recently have I realized what courage it took to do what they did and the trauma it must have caused them.

Their hope was to find Jim in a local hospital, since there were reports of recently rescued survivors who were severely injured or even unconscious. Like Jim, many had no identification on them: Jim's routine at work was to keep his wallet inside his briefcase, not his pants pocket. Maybe, just maybe, Jim was still alive but unable to contact us. It was our last resort, our final grasp at hope.

Maria, Tom, and Loree searched every hospital they could access, but to no avail. They couldn't get close to the disaster area, for the dust and debris in the air were too thick. They had difficulty seeing, difficulty breathing, difficulty finding their way around in the chaos. More than anything, they had difficulty believing that this devastation was real, that the world was now forever changed, and that Jim was gone.

But they also returned with heartwarming stories of kind people and strangers pulling together, helping each other and reaching out with overwhelming love and strength and compassion. One story was about a NYPD policeman. Maria, Tom, and Loree, who knew almost nothing about getting around Manhattan, asked this policeman for directions to several area hospitals and explained their mission to find Jim. The policeman immediately flagged down a Port Authority bus and gave the driver instructions to take the three wherever they needed to go.

This is just one of the countless stories of the spirit that prevailed in New York City in the days following the tragedy. Every story lacks hatred, anger, or vengeance, replaced by a remarkable display of the spirit of humanity at its finest. When Maria, Tom and Loree came home, they agreed with the public's opinion: "We have seen evil at its worst, but goodness at its best."

And so the first days passed ever so slowly...an hour felt like a week, and a day felt like an eternity. The cards, letters, gifts, flowers, phone calls, and visitors were never ending, but no word about Jim. I tried to mentally prepare myself for a phone call from the medical examiner, telling me that they had identified Jim's remains. But that phone call has never come, and deep down I'm thankful I was spared that grief.

I've developed a new philosophy. I only dread one day at a time.

~Charlie Brown

Another
Xanax Day

5

About a week
after the attack, Maria gently suggested to me that we needed to
start thinking about a memorial service for Jim.

I replied simply, "Yes, I know." And that marked the end of
our search and our hope. It was time to make Jim's death official.

On September 28, 2001, in the same church where we had
been married five years before, the same church where we stood
next to each other every Sunday, holding hands and professing
our faith to God, I sat with both families, trembling and sobbing
uncontrollably, as we said goodbye to Jim. It was one of the most
surreal moments of my life. I looked at the altar and the display
of flowers surrounding a 16 × 20 portrait of Jim on an easel, the
tables filled with pictures of him and our life together, and I
could not believe this was happening.

*Wait a minute, didn't we just get married here? It seems like
yesterday that we stood right there, committing our lives to each
other with our wedding vows. How could this happen? This is
not the way it was supposed to be.*

Over six hundred people attended the Mass. Over six hundred people stood in an endless line to offer their condolences.
Over six hundred people showed an outpouring of love, respect,
and admiration for Jim and genuine sympathy. The whole event

was a complete blur for me — a Xanax day if ever there was one. But I think back on it, and I feel honored that so many people cared so much for Jim and that they waited in line for hours to show it. Many of his colleagues from the computer industry traveled quite a distance to pay their respects. This was the first time I had met most of them, but Jim had told me so much about them. It was an emotionally exhausting day, but it did my heart good to see all those faces speaking so highly of the man I love so dearly.

I had never been surrounded by more people in my life. Yet I have never felt so alone.

·tf·

We're in our favorite restaurant, The Grenville. Jim knows few things make me happier than a Grenville dessert.

We've been dating for three months. The "L" word is in play. Recently, Jim has started using the "M" word.

After Chateaubriand for two, Barney, the maitre'd, comes to take our dessert order.

"I'll have the crème brûlée." My mouth is already watering. Jim goes for the caramel flan.

Barney and Jim exchange a look. Is my sweet tooth that obvious?

Fifteen minutes later, I'm wondering why our dessert hasn't arrived and why Jim is so fidgety. I'm about to find out.

Barney sneaks up from behind with my dessert. Right in the middle of the crème brûlée, fresh raspberries, whipped cream, and drizzled chocolate is the most beautiful diamond ring I've ever seen nestled in its box.

I gasp so loud people turn to look at us.

Barney says, "Congratulations!" Jim blushes. My eyes begin to tear.

Jim says, "I've loved you from the first day we met, and I want to spend the rest of my life with you. Will you marry me?"

I blurt out a, "Yes!" and we kiss with an excitement and joy like never before.

Onlookers cheer.

What Dreams
May Come

6

Jim and I were movie buffs. We'd often have full conversations using nothing but lines from different movies.

I'd say, "I'm going to K-Mart. You need anything?"

He'd say, "No. K-Mart sucks." (Dustin Hoffman, *Rain Man*)

I'd reply, "Inconceivable!" (Vizzini, *The Princess Bride*)

He'd finish with, "You can't handle the truth!" (Jack Nicholson, *A Few Good Men*)

We'd make complete sense to each other — and probably no one else. But it was fun and challenging, and we cracked ourselves up trying to outdo each other. We had some sentimental favorites — like *Braveheart*, the first movie we ever saw together. Jim would seduce me with Mel Gibson's fake Scottish brogue: "Ey love yeh. Olways 'ave. Wonna marry yeh." If I nagged him too much, Jim would accuse me of being a Sally: "You're the worst kind. You're high maintenance, but you *think* you're low maintenance" (Billy Crystal, *When Harry Met Sally*). We both know the entire script of *Apollo 13* word-for-word. Our DVD collection is bursting at the seams. Blockbuster rents movies from *us*.

What Dreams May Come is a movie I thought a lot about soon after September 11th. Woman loses her husband (played by

Robin Williams) and both children in a tragic car accident. She's completely alone. Husband and children are in Heaven. Wife can't deal with pain and grief anymore, commits suicide. Wife goes to Hell. Husband spends rest of movie trying to find Wife in Hell and take her to Heaven with him and the kids. This being Hollywood, of course he overcomes all obstacles and returns with her to Heaven. Credits roll. (Sorry if I ruined it for you.)

New Jersey is a long way from Hollywood. And the Black Hole that the Wife jumped into was becoming more tempting than it was scary. But if I killed myself, it would be my luck that I'd go to Hell and Jim would be in Heaven, and then for sure I'd never see him again. Or he'd try like Robin Williams to find me, and we'd both end up spending eternity in Hell. I'm not giving full credit to Hollywood for preventing my suicide, but it did shed some light on a subject that I began to wrestle with — and others suspected it.

A few weeks after September 11th, while dancing around the Black Hole, I went into my nightstand drawer, where my "stash" of medications were kept. Pharmacists tend to accumulate an apothecary's smorgasbord, pills for all occasions — let's just leave it at that. On that day I was looking for a simple Advil for my monster headache, but the drawer was completely empty.

After a screaming fit of, "WHERE ARE MY BOTTLES," my sister Maria (a nurse) and my boss Rich (also a pharmacist) confessed that they had raided the drawer and had taken possession of its contents. I later discovered that Rich had also gone into my purse and taken my keys to the pharmacy. Guess they didn't have much confidence in me. Now that I look back, that was a very wise move on their part. They recognized that I knew exactly which pills — and exactly how many of them — to take as a very permanent solution to my pain. They recognized that I was not making rational decisions and that the potential for another tragedy existed. They recognized that I was too close to the edge of the Black Hole.

tf

Docking our twenty-four-foot bow rider after a day on the river. Jim begins to tie off the stern. I decide to impress him with my newly acquired knowledge of knots. I lean out over the bow and stretch my short arms as far as I can to reach the mooring post. Just a little farther...

Splash! Head first into the black water.

Jim races to the bow, eyes wide, mouth open in disbelief. I fill the awkward silence with —

"GET ME OUT OF HERE!"

I'm imagining the slime and the creatures and the barnacles and foam of unknown origin surrounding me. Jim grabs my wrists, helps me up the ladder, and I flop like a fish back into the boat.

My hero. I've been saved from the Swamp Thing.

Always the diver, Jim's only question is: "So, how was the vis' down there?"

The
Black Hole

7

Because I'm a scuba diver, my vision of the Black Hole is a deep, dark body of water that invites you to take the plunge, promising relief in its depths. This can be very tempting, especially at your most desperate moments. If you allow yourself to dive into this black abyss of depression and despair, you must know how hard it will be to ever climb out again, even when your family and friends try to rescue you. They may throw you a life preserver, but if you're in too deep, if you're too far below the surface, it will not reach you.

Imagine you're a scuba diver, with twenty-one pounds of lead around your waist. You're low on air, and your buoyancy control vest is no longer working. You chose to make this dive, and now you're helplessly sinking faster and faster, deeper and deeper.

This depression, like the lead, will consume your life and drown you if you let it. And I assure you, as a pharmacist, there ain't no pill on Earth that can pull you out of the Black Hole once you're in too deep. You could literally drown in your grief, and you alone are the one who has control over whether this happens or not.

Losing someone you love, especially under tragic and sudden circumstances, shatters your life. The trauma and pain are overwhelming, the feeling of loss terrifying. As a defense mechanism in the first days and weeks after the attack, I felt numb and dazed, in a state of shock, in another dimension. I remember repeating, "This can't be happening!" out loud, over and over and over. This state of denial occasionally turned into outbursts of anger and violent rage — mostly directed toward my poor, helpless family and friends. And throughout it all, I would cry uncontrollably. I was already swimming near the Black Hole — in danger of sinking and not even knowing it.

I could not eat. I had absolutely no appetite for weeks, and when I did attempt to eat something, the food would evacuate itself from my body in some fashion. I could not sleep. Sleep was a scary thing, because it meant eventually waking up again. And waking up meant that this whole thing was not a dream. I wanted to go to sleep forever, never to wake up again. My doctor prescribed Xanax, which I took for a short time. But my knowledge of sedatives and antidepressants provided me with "too much information." I didn't want to become dependent on tranquilizers. As a pharmacist, I've witnessed many patients unable to function without them. I didn't want to go from being a respected pharmacist to a widow to a sleeping pill addict.

I knew I wasn't thinking clearly; in fact, I wasn't thinking at all. I confess that in the first few weeks after 9/11, I gave in to the temptation of taking two, or three, or four Xanax at one time. That's when my sister confiscated my stash. It was then that I realized I was on the road to dependency, and that soon there wouldn't be enough Xanax in the Western Hemisphere to supply my habit...and that simply was not acceptable. I stopped.

34

As for antidepressants, half the world is taking them, and many people shouldn't be. I would like to make this point for the surviving loved ones of other victims: Usually, the cause of bereavement depression is *not* a chemical imbalance, which is what these drugs should be used for. Antidepressants are used for clinical depression — that is, symptoms of depression that you cannot pinpoint a true cause for. If you have persistent feelings of sadness and a loss of enjoyment that interferes with your daily life and there is nothing you can blame it on (such as the loss of a loved one, a stressful job, poor health, etc.), then there could be a chemical imbalance in your brain that can be treated successfully with antidepressants.

But I knew the cause of my depression was something no drug could fix. In fact, antidepressants could have made it worse. If the neurotransmitters in my brain were normal and in balance, (unfortunately, there's no blood test to confirm this) and I took Zoloft or Prozac or Paxil (pick one from the abundance of ssri's — Selective Serotonin Reuptake Inhibitors), the drugs could throw off the balance and cause the neurotransmitters to shift abnormally, causing unwanted side effects and adverse reactions. I was already going through enough emotional turmoil. Why would I want to screw around with the chemicals in my brain? Allow me to also add that some medical professionals hold the opposite view: They argue that severe emotional trauma can itself be the cause of a chemical imbalance in the brain that can be treated successfully with an ssri.

But in my heart I knew there was no pill that would make the pain of grief go away. Believe me, if there was, it would be accessible to me and I'd be taking it. For me, the key to staying away from the edge of the Black Hole was therapy, not drugs. All kinds of therapy. Therapy of private counseling or support groups or both. Therapy of family and friends who truly cared about me and would do anything for me. Therapy of finding something — anything — to keep me busy, so I didn't become consumed with the obvious. Therapy of staying physically healthy, while trying to regain my mental and emotional health. Therapy of doing everything in my power to reclaim control of my life. Therapy of faith and a belief system that trusted God and His Word. Therapy of finding something to look forward to.

Indeed, the Black Hole is easy to fall into, but we have the power to resist it. I learned to recognize the thoughts and actions that pushed me toward the edge and to use every ounce of my energy to avoid them. I found people and things that pulled me away from the edge toward safety, and I depended on them. I held onto the life preserver with everything I had.

Most of all, I learned that we are stronger than we think.

My soul has been deprived of peace...I have forgotten what happiness is. My strength and my future have perished, and so has my Hope in the Lord...

~Lamentations 3: 17-18 (paraphrase)

"God, How
Dare You!"

8

I grew up with a solid religious foundation. I've always believed in God, always tried to do the "right" thing, always went to church every Sunday. I was a nice little Catholic girl.

I was also a spoiled brat.

Sure, my parents spoiled me. I was deprived of nothing as a child, but I also recognized how fortunate I was, although I don't tell Mom and Dad often enough how grateful I am and how much I appreciate them.

But God spoiled me more than they did. Time after time I would pray for something and my prayer would be answered. I always got my way.

Please God, help me pass the Pharmacy Boards.

I passed.

Please God, don't let me be pregnant.

I'm not.

Please God, let this mortgage be approved.

It was.

Please God, heal my brother, Anthony, who has a terminal brain tumor.

He's still going strong.

Please God, help my mom through this surgery.

39

She's fine.

Please God, find me someone to spend my life with. Please let me meet my soul mate to share love and happiness.

Jim Sands appeared.

So, I'm a spoiled brat in a toy store. Everything I ask for, I get. And now, here in front of me is the biggest, the best, the most incredibly important toy in my life, and I absolutely must have it. The towers are burning, and my dear husband is inside. I don't care about anything else, but this is the toy I absolutely must have:

Please, God, bring Jim home.

And just like the spoiled brat who hears the word "No" for the first time, I throw a fit. A tantrum. A full-scale protest to God.

HOW DARE YOU?!

I cursed Him. I shook my fists at Him. I could not imagine why He would take away the most important person in my life.

I could not sleep at night, so I spent those hours yelling at Him, cursing him out loud. I was pissed, big time. I felt gypped. (I still feel gypped.) I felt like He had teased me:

Here, Jennifer. Here's the guy you've been looking for your whole life. Hope you enjoyed your time together. Now I have to take him back. Sorry.

I would shout out loud: "How dare You?! We were happy. We were in love. LOVE, you know, that thing You say is the most important concept for mankind? And You take it away? Just like that? What did Jim ever do to You, God? He believed in You. He was good, true, honest, kind, generous, faithful. What kind of a God are You anyway?

"Okay, maybe You didn't cause this to happen. But allowing

it to happen makes You just as guilty in my book. You allowed him to suffer a horrible death. And now You're allowing me to suffer a horrible life. That's just great. And the worst part of all: I prayed to You to keep him safe. I prayed to You. Every single morning, including that one. Did I not pray hard enough? Or was I not specific enough? Should I have prayed to protect Jim from terrorist attacks? Was that my mistake? I trusted You. I believed that You would not let anything bad happen to him. This is so unfair, so unfair."

And so it went, night after night — screaming matches with my Creator after my family left me alone. Profanities that would make a sailor blush. Anger that began to burn a hole inside my heart.

I was never angry with the terrorists, as difficult as that is to believe. I'm still not angry with them. My anger was completely directed at God. After all, I prayed to God to protect Jim. I did not pray to Osama Bin Laden to please not commit that awful act of violence. I believed and trusted in God. The terrorists — as insane and unjustified as they were — believed and trusted in their own deranged leader, and in their own distorted religion. As crazy and inhumane as their violence was, they believed they were doing the right thing. But did God believe the terrorists were doing the right thing? Did God believe He was doing the right thing by not stopping them? So my anger boiled over for months. I took this very personally. I refused to go to church anymore. I didn't pray anymore.

Instead I cursed Him. Snarled at Him. Spat at Him. Even gave God the finger.

Most people don't truly analyze their relationship with God until it appears that God has failed them. Tragedies are a fork in the road of faith: Tragic events will either make you turn your back on God and abandon faith — or they will bring you closer to Him.

Two months after the tragedy, I was still standing at the fork, seriously considering the darker road.

We're under water with our Cayman divemaster Elke on a reef called "Japanese Garden" — the dive site with the longest underwater tunnel on the island. We can't wait to swim through it, even though we're only novices.

Jim is wearing a new mask. He always has difficulty clearing his masks, inevitably inhaling water through his nose in the process. He calls this his "mask impediment," and like every obstacle in his life, he's determined to overcome it.

We explore the dark, narrow tunnel of coral, fascinated with the vibrant colors that flash all around us as our lights illuminate the walls. Yellow-tail snappers flit by as we swim through the passage at a depth of sixty feet.

Elke emerges first, followed by me, then Jim. We turn to watch Jim as he kneels in the sand outside the tunnel's exit and signals that his mask is leaking. He pulls out his spare and, without any hesitation, removes his new mask and replaces it with his old standby. He clears it to remove all the water, then gives the "Okay" sign.

So much for impediments.

Angels
from Above

9

Just as I was struggling with the darkest evils of my life, a series of strangers entered my world and guided me away from the Black Hole. They showed me a way back to God and a life worth living. I call them my "angels from above." Some of them I've met in person; others I still only know through letters, e-mails, and phone calls. But each of these strangers entered my life unexpectedly and drastically changed my thinking.

The first two were Willem and Ethel.

Flashback to November 1999 on the tiny island of Bonaire, fifty miles off the Caribbean coast of Venezuela. Bonaire's license plate says it all: "Diver's Paradise." Jim and I were on a boat with twelve other divers, getting ready to dive a site called "Forest." The water seemed exceptionally choppy with a strong current. Although Jim was fine with the conditions, I became nervous about the dive and said so to the divemaster, Willem, who assured me this was just surface chop and that the water would be as calm as a bathtub once we descended past five feet. I wasn't convinced, and

I hounded him about this. Willem became uncharacteristically quiet, then leaned over and whispered in my ear in his soft Papiamento accent, "Do not worry. I am your angel sent from above. I will not leave you." This sent a chill down my spine, and I immediately trusted him.

Willem was true to his word. The current disappeared just as he predicted, yet he still never left my side, guiding Jim and me on a personal tour of this magical reef named after the thickets of black coral trees that turn the underwater reef slope into a wilderness. I never forgot Willem for his kindness and his gift of "Forest." We gave him our e-mail address when we left the island and told him to keep in touch. We never heard from him, but we visited Bonaire several times after that and always made a point to say hello to my angel, Willem.

In January 2001, we traveled to Bonaire once again. Of course we didn't know it then, but this would be our last time on the island. We were asked by the underwater videographer of the dive shop to be "actors" in the making of a dive orientation video about Bonaire. Watching the video would be a requirement for any diver who rented tanks from this dive operation. We gladly accepted and had great fun pulling off Academy Award-worthy performances of renting gear, assembling equipment, doing beach entries, and all the rest. The video wouldn't be completed until after we left the island, so we would have to wait until our next trip to see ourselves on film.

Our next trip to Bonaire was scheduled for November 2001. When September 11th changed those plans, I had to call the airlines and hotel to cancel. These were extremely difficult and emotional phone calls to make, but everyone I spoke with was sympathetic and cooperative. Yet the calls broke my heart. Jim and I were supposed to be adding more happy memories to our growing collection. We had something to look forward to. We were going to see ourselves as the stars of the dive orientation video. Now, I thought, I would never get to see it.

Word of Jim's death spread on Bonaire from the hotel to the dive shop. Willem, who remembered us and had kept our e-mail address from years before, contacted me. He was so sorry for what had happened, and he wanted to send me a copy of the dive video. I was thrilled, honored, and so grateful. Willem proved once again that he really was my angel sent from above. After I received the tape, I watched it alone, crying and laughing and wishing so badly that Jim was there watching it with me.

He should be here. This isn't how it's supposed to be.

Enter Willem's wife Ethel, who came into my life at a time when my anger toward God was at its peak, and my faith seriously shaken. I didn't realize it then, but I was headed down a road of anger and bitterness that would have consumed my life the way it has the lives of others touched by the 9/11 tragedy.

Ethel turned me around.

She and I began e-mailing each other on a regular basis, although we had never met before. Soon I saw how her faith was as strong as a rock, and I began to open up to her. Ethel would listen quietly as I vented my anger toward God. I felt great comfort in pouring out my feelings to this virtual stranger. Most of all, I came to value and depend on her words and her wisdom. She made some strong spiritual points, and I thought about them long and hard. My mind eventually became clearer and clearer...and my anger lessened. I began to cool off.

Ethel helped me to understand that God knew I was angry and why. God expected me to be angry with Him. He created me. He knew my every thought and word. I didn't have to yell and curse at Him. He already knew how I felt. Most of all, He felt bad too.

I realized that I had to make a critical decision: Did I really

47

believe in God? Or was faith merely a two-thousand-year-old concept fabricated to help us cope better with the trials of life? Was there really an eternity called Heaven, or was Heaven just another fabrication to help us cope with the loss of someone we dearly love? I live only an hour away from Atlantic City, but I've never been a gambler. Now I had to decide whether or not to put all my chips on the table. I must bet it all, or nothing. There was no "maybe," no room for gray areas, not when my life and eternity were at stake.

With Ethel's help I realized something that helped turn my life around: My anger with God was proof that I still believed He existed. Otherwise, I couldn't be angry with Him. It became clear to me — I wasn't questioning God's existence. I was questioning His actions. I was questioning the wisdom of His plan. I was questioning the reason for this madness. I was questioning why He didn't answer my prayers.

But, I was not questioning the existence of God Himself.

When it's my turn to meet God face-to-face, we have a lot of things to discuss. We are going to sit down over a cup of Starbuck's mocha cappuccino and biscotti (I'm sure He'll be able to arrange this), and He is going to explain to me exactly why things had to happen the way they did. Maybe He'll say, "Shut up and just be glad you got in the door." Maybe He'll present it like the movie, *It's A Wonderful Life*, and I'll get to see what my fate would have been under different circumstances — say, if Jim had lived, but was permanently disabled. Or if Jim had died in a different way. Or if I had died first and left Jim with a nightmare.

As for my prayers not being answered that fateful day, that

bothered me for a long time. But Ethel told me God always answers our prayers. He's just very creative in the way He does it. He answers them according to His will, not our wishes. So I thought about this, and it finally hit me: God really did answer my prayers that fateful morning. I asked God to get Jim to work safely, and He did. I asked God to bring Jim home. And He did that too...but to His Home, not ours.

Very creative.

So my anger toward God started out in bitterness:

How dare You? You could have stopped this from happening, and You didn't.

It eventually subsided from anger to disappointment:

I just don't understand, God. Why, please tell me why, why, why...

And in time, it got downgraded even further to acceptance:

Okay, if this is Your will, I don't have much choice but to accept it. I don't have to like it, but I will accept it. Just help me get through it, that's all.

After spending time and effort searching for answers — answers that I will never receive until the day I stand before Him — I have finally cooled myself down to the optimal temperature: I trust God. I trust Him with everything I do, with everything I have, with everything I am.

I trust that He will take care of me for the rest of my life. "Do not worry about tomorrow, for tomorrow will take care of itself." (Matthew 6:34 NASB)

I trust that He's got something up His sleeve for me. "For I know the plans I have for you...to give you hope, and a future." (Jeremiah 29:11 NIV)

I trust that He will be there with me, no matter how deep the water is. "I will never leave you, nor forsake you." (Joshua 1:5 NIV)

I trust that He will comfort me and ease all my worries and

fears. "Cast your anxieties upon Him, because He cares for you." (1 Peter 5:7 NIV)

I trust. I believe. I also accept this:

God never promised us that our faith would protect us from pain and struggles and burdens. But He does promise that He'll give us strength to get through them and that He'll be right there with us every step of the way. So I can face the waves, because I know The One who created the ocean.

Oh, and by the way, I have a new prayer that I say every morning without fail:

Lord, remind me that nothing is going to happen to me today that you and I together can't handle.

We're on the sofa, my head in Jim's lap, watching Tom Hanks in Castaway. It's toward the end of the movie after Hanks is rescued after five years on an island by himself. He returns to America only to find his former fianceé married with a young daughter.

"I hate this part of the movie," Jim says.

"Me too. The poor guy does everything in his power to survive, just so he can be reunited with the love of his life."

"She sure didn't waste any time hookin' up with that dentist and havin' a kid. I could never do that."

"Yeah, I could never move on that quickly."

We look at each other. Then we both say the same exact words, simultaneously:

"I'm not sure I could ever move on!"

Something to Look Forward to

10

The Greek playwright Euripedes once said, "There is something in the pang of change, More than the heart can bear, Unhappiness remembering happiness..." Wow. *Unhappiness remembering happiness.* That pretty much sums it up for me during the weeks leading up to Thanksgiving 2001. The fact that I could be so happy one minute and so unhappy the next still blows my mind.

I dreaded that Thanksgiving — the first major holiday without Jim. Like all reminders of my former happiness, I knew it would hurt. My goal back then became to make these reminders hurt less and less, and in time they have. In the beginning, people would attempt to console me with, "Oh, but at least you have such wonderful memories of your time together," and I'd want to clock them for saying it. Didn't they understand? Memories hurt. They are powerful and painful to recall. Memories sting, they taunt, they tease, they torture, they remind me over and over: You'll never do that again, at least not with Jim.

Before 9/11, my mind would occasionally drift off to one of our previous dive vacations — very happy times — and I'd think to myself, *I can't wait to go back.* The anticipation of going back was almost as great as the vacation itself. The anticipation would ultimately become reality, and then reality became another great memory to add to our collection. After 9/11, I could never again add memories to that collection. Memories with Jim had become finite, a dead end street.

In the beginning, I found it so painful to even think about our good times together that I completely blocked them out — a defense mechanism, a protective device to keep me from having a meltdown. In time, I was able to recall them, but a heavy sadness would come over me and linger:

There's nothing to look forward to. Nothing but a big, fat, empty, lonely future.

It was in this frame of mind that I stumbled upon one of the keys to getting through the nightmare: finding *something to look forward to*. Without it, life seemed overwhelmingly empty with no end in sight. It was the anticipation factor that was missing. It was having a concrete event — big or small — to look ahead to and wish for it to come faster.

For me, another complete stranger by the name of David Taylor, executive editor of *Rodale's Scuba Diving* magazine, provided me with one of my most important healing tools. He provided me with the first *something to look forward to* at a time when it was intensely needed — the winter holidays of 2001 — and proved to be powerfully therapeutic.

Jim was a budding underwater photographer, and a very good one at that. He loved to capture beautiful and interesting marine life on film, and it became his passion. He never had any formal instruction in underwater photography; he read books and magazines and relied on the trial and error of practice. Some of his photographs were stunningly professional, and I had many of them enlarged, framed, and hung in our house. I even made him sign them in the event he'd be famous one day. Jim often commented, half-jokingly, about his desire to have his photos published in a dive magazine. I knew this would be a dream come true for him, but I also knew how humble he was about it when I encouraged him to send some in. He would just shrug his shoulders and make that "I don't know" face.

As Thanksgiving 2001 approached, two months after the tragedy, I was losing my mind, out of control with despair and grief. Nothing could make me happy; no one could make me smile. I remember standing in the foyer of my house, staring blankly at Jim's beautiful framed underwater photos and wishing so desperately for his embrace or just to hear his voice say, "I should have used my macro lens on that one."

Then it hit me.

I needed to do something for him, to show him how much I love him, to show people just what a remarkable person he was. I wanted to make his dream come true: I wanted to have his photographs published in his favorite dive magazine, *Rodale's Scuba Diving*. We had subscriptions to four different diving magazines, but *Rodale's* was the one Jim enjoyed and respected the most.

I began "The Crusade": I wrote a letter to David Taylor, the executive editor, and included several of Jim's best photos. I imagined this would be a tough mission; magazines have limited space and typically only publish photographs by professionals. I mentally prepared myself for a disappointing reply such as: "We're sorry for your loss, Mrs. Sands, but we just cannot accommodate his photos, yadda yadda yadda." I might even have to go to plan B, although I had no clue what that might be.

Instead of "yaddas," however, I received a warm, sincere, and sympathetic letter from David himself, who was touched by the story and considered it a "privilege to share Jim's talent and passion for underwater photography." David even asked me to send more of Jim's photos to use on Rodale's web site (www.scubadiv-ing.com). I remember crying when I read David's letter — and for the first time in three months, I was crying out of happiness, not grief.

David told me Jim's story and his photos would appear in the March 2002 issue of *Rodale's Scuba Diving*. And so, from November to March, I had *something to look forward to*, an antici-pation of something good.

Indeed, Jim's photos were published, both in the magazine and on the web site, where Jim was named "Photographer of the Week" and his pictures appeared along with David's story about Jim titled "An American Hero." It made me feel happy — a truly foreign concept at that time — knowing how proud Jim would have been (no, how proud he is) to see that his dream had come true. It was such an incredible tribute and gift to Jim, to honor him in this way. And for those months before and after the March 2002 issue, I depended heavily on this tribute to get me through my difficult hours. Whenever I felt myself going near the edge of that Black Hole or on the verge of a meltdown, I forced myself to think about Jim's photos in the magazine and on the web site, then I forced myself to imagine Jim's proud and beaming smile as he watched from above. I forced myself to real-ize that there was, once again, *something to look forward to*.

Priceless therapy, indeed.

It's the afternoon of May 4, 2001, our fifth wedding anniversary. We're scuba diving in Cayman, swimming with all of our fish friends. Jim takes a metal carabiner clip and bangs on his tank to get my attention. Then he points to his watch and holds up three fingers — "Three o'clock," he's signaling.

This marks the actual time we said our marriage vows. My heart is about to burst with love for him. He removes the regulator from his mouth, takes my hand, and kisses it. Then he pulls out his dive slate and writes in big letters:

"I DO."

Reality
Bricks

11

They were cement blocks falling from the sky and crashing on my head. I might be doing pretty good, considering the cards I'd been dealt, then something would trigger the knowledge that, indeed, life as I knew it was over.

I call them "reality bricks," and they still fall. Even though I had added a powerful new tool to my therapeutic skill set — *something to look forward to* — I also learned that reality would always find a way to slap me upside the head as a reminder of September 11th and the end of life as I knew it. Some of the bricks came from other people. Some came by themselves, unbidden. Some came daily. Some still do. Such as:

+ **Waking up every morning and realizing that this is not a dream.**

    For months, I would cry myself to sleep, then upon waking, just as a sliver of consciousness forced its way in, even though my eyes were still closed — BAM! — a reality brick dropped like an anvil. Then came the thought suddenly, like a knife at my throat —

    It really happened. He's not lying next to me. He never will be again. He is dead.

59

So I'd cry myself awake. The days began and ended with tears. The mornings were always — and still are — the worst part of my day. I still have to force myself to get out of bed each morning, dreading the fact that I must face yet another day without Jim.

• Every holiday, birthday, and anniversary.
It's the classic "Empty Chair Syndrome." The fact is made blatantly obvious by the occasion that someone is missing, someone who is supposed to be there but will never arrive.

• A familiar song on the radio or the smell of the men's cologne, Polo.
Emotional land mines, just waiting for me to stumble upon them.

• Reading Jim's obituary in the newspaper.
When I wrote it, I was definitely on mental autopilot. I simply summed up his thirty-eight years into four paragraphs, scanned a decent photo of him, and sent it to the newspaper via cyberspace, as if I was sending someone a recipe or something. It just wasn't real until I saw it in the newspaper a few days later. Seeing it in print on the daily page dedicated to World Trade Center victims, that's when the brick hit — and it was a big one.

• Shopping for greeting cards.
I realized that I'd never buy another husband card again, nor would I ever again receive a wife card.

• Every time I see a bottle of Pepto Bismol.

If only that stuff didn't work so well. If only it hadn't worked at all, and his stomach was still so upset in the morning that he had called in sick...or went in late...or something...or anything.

◆ **The first time I read his death certificate and saw the cause of death: Homicide.**

Seeing that word in print added insult to injury to a degree I didn't expect. I guess a lot of my reality bricks don't fall from the sky as spoken words or familiar events. Some of them are unbearably agonizing words on a page, words like "widow," "remains," and "homicide" — tossed like hand grenades into my lap.

◆ **Jim's laptop computer.**

Every month reminders pop up for his allergy shots and his hair cut. He must have them hard-coded in the system, because I can't turn off the alarms. I keep his laptop continually up and running. I can't bring myself to turn it off or disconnect it, even though I never use it. I feel like that would be "pulling the plug" on him, which would be an even bigger reality brick. I have no intention of ever shutting down his computer. He saved every e-mail I ever sent him. Foolishly, I did not.

◆ **Seeing or hearing jets flying at low altitudes.**

We live between McGuire Air Force Base and the Newark, New Jersey airport. Flight plans often take military and commercial planes directly over our district. It sends a chill down my spine every time and instantly displays an image in my head that I prefer not to remember.

✦ Opening his closet or dresser drawers.

At the time of this writing, I avoid doing either. And if I absolutely have to go in there, I have a meltdown. Right there on the spot. A big part of this is what I call "olfactory overload." His clothes still smell like him, so if I open Jim's closet, I get slammed with a scent that triggers a nerve in my brain, and that nerve triggers another nerve, which fools me into thinking — for a split second — that Jim is there in the room with me. Then that nerve triggers the reality nerve, and the whole thing goes downhill from there with bricks flying everywhere.

✦ Seeing the New York skyline.

I don't know which brick hits harder: a picture of the towers in their glory days or the emptiness of the skyline as it appears now.

✦ Watching Jim's Lexus get towed away from our house.

Jim had just leased a new Lexus when he started the job with eSpeed. He truly loved that car and enjoyed driving it. We figured since he was spending so much time on the road, he needed a comfortable car that he would get pleasure from driving. After September 11th, my finances wouldn't allow me to keep both vehicles; besides, I had no use for two anyway. I decided to keep my suv for the Northeast's bad weather and arranged a voluntary repossession of the Lexus.

I had the dismal task of cleaning out Jim's car to prepare it for pickup. All I could think of was how Jim could not have known, as he drove to work that morning, that his life was about to end. Everything inside the car seemed so normal, as if nothing had happened. His favorite Red Sail Sports dive jacket was still on the front passenger seat. His travel mug still in that nifty cup holder — coffee still in it. His gum wrappers and tissues stuffed in the ashtray. All his favorite music loaded in the CD changer. Everything just as it should be. Just one thing missing. The driver.

It was an unusually warm day in October when the tow truck pulled into the driveway. My mom and I stood outside and watched as the driver rigged up the car, expressed his condolences, and drove away — with Jim's beloved Lexus trailing behind. It felt like I was losing Jim all over again.

◆ **The day I took my very last birth control pill.**

I won't forget that one. I stayed on The Pill for a few months after September 11th because I knew that if I stopped them immediately, the combination of my unstable emotional state and my roller coaster estrogen would send me into hormonal anarchy. So I continued to take my pill every morning, and that reality brick hurt so badly each time I swallowed it. *Here I go again, taking a pill for which I now have absolutely no use whatsoever. I will never again make love to my husband.* So on the morning of December 16th, I sat on the edge of my bed and popped out the very last Ortho Novum from its blister pack, calmly swallowed it with a sip of water from my Poland Spring water bottle, put the cap back on, and sat there for a minute. Then the Brick hit. And in an explosive rage, I flung that bottle of water harder than I have ever thrown anything in my life. It hit the wall and burst, water splashing everywhere, mixing with the tears of my pain. And I thought: *There's nothing on this earth I would not do just to touch him again or see him again. Nothing.*

63

tf

We're in TGI Friday's on our first date. We still can't understand how it's possible that we don't know each other despite having lived only blocks apart our entire lives.

Jim says, "I can't believe it. I drive past your house all the time. I always look at it and think to myself, 'What kind of person would live in a house with a pink door?'"

I think to myself, Maybe you, one day.

The Husband Card

12

One way that I gauge my recovery is by realizing that reality bricks are falling less often now and are not hurting as much when they land. In the very beginning, there were crash landings every hour or so. Then every few hours. Then once or twice a day. Then a few times a week. And as time passed, the landings got softer. There's still a thud, but the pain is not as intense. Some reality bricks hurt more than others: I can deal with Jim's hair cut reminders, but I still can't go in his closet. I've even confronted one of them head on: the husband greeting cards.

Jim and I kept Hallmark in business. For every special occasion, or sometimes for no reason at all, we'd buy multiple cards for each other and hide them all over the house. In the refrigerator, in his brief-case, by my toothbrush, in the car. Thankfully, I saved every one of them (so did he). The very last card that he gave me was for the anniversary of our engagement. Inside it he wrote: "I remember the emptiness you filled when we met, and I cannot imagine my life without you." Three weeks later, I was forced to remember that emptiness myself, and I was forced to live *my* life without *him*.

Then one day I was shopping in Target for a birthday card for my father — and there they were, practically jumping out at me, furiously trying to get my attention: the dreaded husband cards. I couldn't look at them. I refused. They were like daggers. Reality bricks coming at me from all directions. But they were also right next to the father cards. How could I ignore them? Then I saw a husband card with a cool tropical fish on the front. Oh, how Jim would have loved that! Dare I look inside? No, I'll have a meltdown, right here in the store. But I have to look, it's killing me. I pick it up. I open it.

"Happy Birthday to my husband, the catch of a lifetime."

I snap it closed. *Ugh.* The perfect card for him. *This is so unfair.* Then I feel the tears starting to come. My throat closes up, and suddenly I'm wincing, holding back the sobs right there in the middle of a department store with people all around. I take a deep breath. Another one. Okay, tears are streaming down my face, but at least the sobbing is curtailed. More deep breaths. Find a Kleenex, fast. The card is still in my hand. But putting it back means bona fide reality, and might trigger another sobbing outburst that maybe I can't stop. Another deep breath. *Now, think about this. What would be the harm in buying it? So what if Jim isn't here to read it? Or maybe he is, and I just can't see him.*

66   I made a big decision that day. I refused to accept that I would never buy another husband card. I picked up that reality brick and hurled it right back. Since that day, I have bought Jim several cards. I spill my

love and grief inside them, hoping that maybe he's looking over my shoulder as I write. I seal the envelope and put them (in an ever-increasing pile) on his nightstand. And now I can shop in the greeting card department freely and without anxiety or dread, having defeated the enemy. My goal is to eventually over-come all the reality bricks, one by one. There are no shortcuts in the grief process, but I have learned this:

You can't get *through* the pain until you *face* the pain.

·tf·

"And now, performing a Viennese waltz and making their first public appearance as husband and wife—Mr. and Mrs. James Sands!" The wedding reception cheers.

Jim and I stride arm-in-arm to the dance floor...the music starts. We've practiced the moves with our dance instructor a thousand times. Can we pull it off now, when it counts?

We begin gliding to the music. One, two, three. One, two, three. Our eyes are glued to each other; we must never look away. Shoulders down. Chin up. Back straight. Smile. One, two, three. Deep breath, here comes the first spin.

"Oh no, Jim, I can't hear the beat," I mutter through my clenched teeth like a ventriloquist. The crowd is cheering so loud we can't hear the music.

"Just follow my lead, hon, we're doin' great," Jim squeezes my hand with each beat, to keep our timing.

Another big spin. Please God, don't let me trip on my gown. The crowd goes wild.

Finally, it's over. Roaring applause. Jim pulls an impromptu move and dips me...then we kiss, a most passionate kiss. "I think I'm gonna pass out..." I pant, out of breath.

"Me too," he says. "Let's do it again."

68

The Rose
and the Lenox Vase

13

On October 8, 2001, less than one month after the worst terrorist attack in our nation's history, another unthinkable tragedy occurred. But this one didn't make the daily headlines, so most people don't even know it even happened.

Sustaining winds of 140 mph, Hurricane Iris ravaged the Caribbean coast of Belize, causing great damage to homes and property, and capsizing the 120-foot live-aboard scuba diving boat, *M.V. Wave Dancer*, owned by Peter Hughes Diving. Twenty passengers aboard the boat drowned, trapped in the flooded cabins of the vessel. The owner of the boat had made the decision not to evacuate the passengers, despite warnings that Iris would slam into Belize with deadly force.

I did not read about the *Wave Dancer* tragedy in the newspaper or see it on television. Instead, I discovered a quarter-page announcement of the deaths in a dive magazine buried among advertisements for scuba gear. My heart broke for their families. I realized that since this accident did not have the same global effect as the September 11th terrorist attacks, the families probably did not experience the degree of assistance that I had, but their grief and their needs could be no less than mine. They did not have the Red Cross and United Way to help them with their financial burdens. All they had was a simple memorial fund that was set up for readers of the magazine to donate to. So I did. I wanted to share the kindness and generosity that the American people had shown me, to "pay it forward" as the Kevin Spacey movie encourages.

After receiving my donation, the wife of one of the victims e-mailed to thank me. Teresa Mars and I have much in common besides the obvious unfortunate circumstances of suddenly and tragically losing our husbands. Turns out that Teresa is a pharmacist too. Like Jim and me, she and her husband Ray enjoyed many dive vacations before his life ended way too soon.

Teresa and I had never met, but we immediately connected. Through the miracles of e-mail, we have created our own private support group for each other. We understand the agony of widowhood from a perspective that no one else in our lives can possibly comprehend. We understand the anxiety of our new lives without our husbands. We can fully relate to the pressures of the pharmacy profession. We help pull each other away from the edge of the Black Hole. We stick together, and we know that we will get through this. We won't ever get *over* it, but we'll get *through* it.

So God has placed yet another angel in the cast of Jennifer's "new life." Another stranger who lives far away, whom I have never met, yet who has proven to be powerfully influential in my recovery. I sent a small check to a good cause. And God repaid me a thousand-fold with Teresa's friendship.

He never ceases to amaze me.

Recently Teresa gave me a fresh outlook on my situation, an illustration in which she often places herself with her beloved Ray. This is what she wrote to me in an e-mail:

Flowers, by themselves, are beautiful.

70

The Rose and the Lenox Vase

> *A vase, displayed by itself, is a work of art.*
>
> *Put the flower inside the vase, and you have perfect unity.*
>
> *But flowers eventually wither and die. A vase is breakable, and there's always the possibility that it will be dropped and shatter into a thousand pieces. Inevitably, one of them will be without the other.*

So I am a rose. Jim is a Lenox vase. Alone, we were lovely, yet incomplete. Together, we made each other shine.

One tragic day, that Lenox vase came crashing to the ground, and so did my heart. As a fragile life form, I will ultimately meet my own fate one day. Until then, I have two choices: I can either become so consumed with my loss that I prematurely wither and dry up, becoming emotionally ugly, a stick of thorns. Or I can allow myself — even force myself, sometimes against my ability — to maintain some degree of control and strength. The rose must be a testimony to the vase, a precious reminder of the life companion who once held her. I want people to say: "You can see how deeply Jennifer and Jim were in love, and you can actually see and feel Jim's surviving spirit inside her...by expressing herself, she expresses Jim too."

The rose really misses the vase. The rose feels even more empty and lonely than she did before she was ever held by the vase. But this flower must bask in the vase's memory, not dwell in its shattered loss.

So, it's taken me a while, but I've finally come to a conclusion: I want to remember Jim for the way he lived, not the way he

71

died. I want to remember every day we had together before September 11th, the day I struggle to put somewhere inaccessible in my head.

But sometimes the world simply won't allow that...

Perfect timing. I take the chicken out of the oven just as Jim walks in the door after his workout. I can tell by the way he's hobbling that he's overdone it — again.

"A few too many jump squats?"

"Yeah, I guess." He's walking like he just had a prostate exam.

"Now you're gonna be crippled tomorrow. Why do you do this to yourself?"

"Twenty-six days to Bonaire. Gotta get rid of this." He pats his belly. "Looks like I'm in my third trimester. Gonna give birth to a basketball."

I roll my eyes. "Okay, hon. Go sit down. Dinner's ready." Instead he heads to the freezer and takes out a pint of Ben and Jerry's ice cream.

"What're you doing?" I ask.

"Taking it out ahead of time, so it'll thaw and I can scoop it easier."

WTCW
and KITA

14

When I started Jim's Lexus to prepare it for repossession, this song from *Aida* burst forth from the CD player — probably the last song Jim heard before his death that morning:

> *You've plundered our wisdom, our knowledge, our wealth...in bleeding us dry, you long for our spirit. But that you will never possess.*

The words are sung by the Nubian King's daughter, Aida, who was just captured as a slave by their enemy, the Egyptian Army. She addresses the song to her captors on behalf of her injured nation. We, as families of the victims, could address her song to the 9/11 terrorists:

You may plunder us, you may long for our spirit, but you will never possess it or us. Never.

Since September 11th, Jim and I have been reduced to abbreviations. I am now officially a WTCW. No, it's not a radio station. I didn't know what it stood for either, the first time I read it. I had to ask someone. I knew WTC stood for World Trade Center, but that second "W" stumped me. I was floored at the answer, slammed by another reality brick out of nowhere:

World Trade Center Widow.

Jim is now officially, "James Sands, Jr., KITA." Killed In Terrorist Attack. I found that one out when I traveled to Jersey City one month after Jim's death to obtain his death certificate. I had to meet with an FBI agent, who informed me of the addition to Jim's name. "KITA" must now be written in red, felt-tip marker at the top of each page of our income tax returns and other legal documents from this day forward.

I understand the necessity of official acronyms in a global disaster such as this, but there's something about them that hits home a little too hard. I feel like we've been branded, like cattle. Do Holocaust survivors write "HS" after their name? What about the Oklahoma City families? And the Challenger and Columbia space shuttle families? I now have lifetime membership in an exclusive club that I did not sign up for, and each time I see WTCW or KITA, a reality brick comes sailing in.

For the first six months after the tragedy, I would receive at least one important letter or document in the mail every day from various government agencies. If it wasn't the Governor of New Jersey, it was the Governor of New York. Or the Senate. Or the House of Representatives. Or the FBI. Or the Mayor of New York. Or the Medical Examiner. Or the New York Crime Victims Board. I would walk down to my mailbox and think, *Hmm...wonder who I'll hear from today?* and take a deep breath as I opened my mailbox. The official and legal aspects were — and still are — overwhelming and downright terrifying.

Documents from the Senate and the House of Representatives involve ongoing information on the Federal Victims Com-

76

pensation Fund. Applying for the fund means families forfeit their right to file private lawsuits against other involved parties, such as the airline industry. The FBI advises me of my rights to protection and privacy, my rights to be notified and to be present at all court proceedings relating to September 11ᵗʰ, and my rights against media harassment. The Department of Justice continually updates me on the trial of Zacarias Moussaoui. The Governor of New Jersey established the 9/11 Family Advocate Program. The Governor of New York and the Mayor of New York City always have something important to say. Recently it's been about the plans to build a permanent memorial at the site of Ground Zero. And everyone has a form for me to fill out and return: "Please provide information on the Victim." For the six hundredth time.

The one envelope that I still dread seeing in my mailbox is from the Office of the Medical Examiner. I have received only a few things from them, and each time I saw the return address, I began to tremble and have difficulty breathing. To date, the ME tells me, none of Jim's "remains" have been found. I detest that word "remains." The only word I hate more is the name of the landfill where they keep the WTC remains: "Freshkill." Incredibly, that's the name of the garbage dump designated as the recovery site for WTC victim remains. What's worse than a reality brick? A reality bomb?

I have convinced myself that it would be better for everyone if nothing at all is ever found of Jim. The method of burial would cause a big family controversy. We've already had his memorial service, and another ceremony — even a private one — would open up that painful wound once again.

Most of all, in the darkest parts of my mind, the places where I dare not go lest I get too close to the edge of the Black Hole, I must believe that Jim died quickly and painlessly, that he didn't

77

even know what was happening. Somehow I justify this belief with the fact that no remains have been found. I could be totally wrong; my theory isn't provable. But the alternative is unthinkable. The thoughts of what the last moments of Jim's life were like: the image of how it looked and felt and sounded when a commercial jetliner was heading straight for the window, eight floors below...the idea that he could have been alive until the time that his tower collapsed...and if so, the desperation he must have felt, knowing there was no way out. These and other haunting visions tear me apart. They are the reason why I will be in therapy for the rest of my life. They are the reason why I must believe that "no remains" is a good thing for me. They are the reason why I must focus on Jim's life, instead of his death, in order to cope and survive.

To appoint unto them that mourn in Zion, to give unto them beauty for ashes, the oil of joy for mourning, the garment of praise for the spirit of heaviness; that they might be called trees of righteousness, the planting of the Lord, that he might be glorified.

~Isaiah 61:3 (KJV)

Constant Reminders, Constant Gratitude

15

Without a doubt, this was the worst terrorist attack in our country's history and, like the bombing of Pearl Harbor by the Japanese, it marks a turning point for our nation and the world. Neither will ever again be the same. The attacks on 9/11 have impacted every person in America, whether or not they lost someone.

Maybe some people think that September 11th is a thing of the past already. It is not. Not for the thousands of grieving families, nor the rescue workers, nor the unemployed and disabled survivors. Not for any of us who relive it like it was yesterday. Not for those of us who cannot forget.

I have struggled with the "We will not forget" anthem that has consumed our nation. Here's the bottom line for me: No, we should not ever forget what happened on that day. But do we have to keep reliving it? Shouldn't this new anthem be expanded to "We will not forget our loved ones" as opposed to the underlying meaning, "We will not forget those burning towers" and "We will not forget to exact our revenge?"

If a person is killed in an automobile accident, the extent of the coverage of the story usually consists of a photo in the local newspaper, possibly a mention of it on the eleven o'clock news. The family of that poor victim would never want to continually

"Grieving Angel," sculpted by Brian Hanlon.
Dedicated August, 2002.
Brick, New Jersey

see the wreckage of the car and the gruesome reminder of the last moments of their loved one's life. It hurts enough seeing it once. But over and over? On every news channel and newspaper for months? It reopens the wound every time. But it's funny how human nature works. People are fascinated with tragedy — violence, fires, accidents, natural disasters, terrorist attacks — as long as no one they know got hurt.

The families of September 11th cannot and will not ever escape the memory of what happened that day. Although the grim novelty has subsided, there are still remnants of it everywhere. It is no longer the headline of the news every day, but there's virtually always a mention of it in some fashion. What kind of a memorial will be built at the site? When are the PATH trains going to run again? What's the latest on the Federal Victim's Compensation Fund? By now, most of the information is benign, as long as it isn't accompanied by a graphic picture or video of the towers collapsing. Oh, right, but then it wouldn't be an interesting story. Gotta have that flashback of a man in a business suit desperately jumping out the window from the 105th floor while the towers burned, just so that "We will not forget." Believe me, his wife will not forget. Can you imagine what she must feel, seeing that? Like me, I bet she has been reduced to watching only the safe channels: HGTV, Game Show Network, and Animal Planet.

Don't get me wrong, I'm not complaining about the abundance of flags and bumper stickers, provided they are respectful and appropriate. The patriotism in this country since that day has been heartwarming and inspirational, and without the support and generosity of the American people, I honestly do not know where I would be right now. And since I'll probably never get an opportunity like this again, here's my chance to thank you all:

To my family... It would be easier to remove the light from the

83

sun than to find the right words. Thank you for holding me up and calming me down. Thank you for constantly being my source of comfort, guidance, wisdom, and support.

To my friends... Thank you for being my psychiatrists, my preachers, my chefs, my secretaries, my chauffeurs, my entertainment, and my advisors. Thank you for being my shoulder to cry on, and for giving me reasons to laugh.

To my neighbors... Thank you for taking care of me during those first few awful months and for continuing to do so. Thank you for feeding me with delicious meals. Thank you for raking my lawn and shoveling my snow...for fixing broken things in my house and for helping to mend a broken heart.

To my co-workers and customers at the pharmacy... Thank you for your never-ending cards, letters, and flowers. Thank you for your sincere thoughts, your constant prayers, your kind words, and your warm hugs.

To all of the September 11th Organizations (including the American Red Cross, United Way, September 11th Fund, and numerous others all across America)... If it were not for your financial support, I would certainly have been in dire straits. The relief you provided immediately following the tragedy was truly a godsend. I was not mentally capable of returning to work right away, and your support covered my mortgage and household expenses until I was able to do so. Thank you for saving my house — and my sanity.

84

To Mayor Scarpelli and the town of Brick, New Jersey... Thank you for dedicating a 9/11 memorial to the victims from our town. "The Grieving Angel" captures our emotions and provides the families with a place to visit and to pay our respects. Thank you, Brian Hanlon, for sculpting such an amazing tribute. Your words describe the angel perfectly: "She's powerful. She's passionate. She's angry. She's doubled over in grief. But when she's strong enough to rise again, she's got some business to take care of."

To New Jersey Governor James McGreevey, U.S. Congressman Chris Smith, State Senator Andrew Ciesla...Thank you for continuing to provide the New Jersey 9/11 families unending support and assistance. Your compassion and sensitivity to our circumstances have been a tremendous comfort and one that we know we can count on.

To every single person in the world who ever contributed to any of the September 11th Organizations...Please know that your donations made my life — and the lives of all the families — easier by relieving our economic burdens. You imagined our distress, and despite your own needs, you selflessly gave of yourselves to lessen ours. Your generosity, kindness, and compassion will never ever be forgotten.

Thank you, U.S. House of Representatives...For flying an American flag in Jim's name at the White House and for sending it to me.

Thank you, NASA...For flying an American flag in Jim's name on the Space Shuttle Endeavor and for sending it to me.

Thank you, Mission Refuel F-18 Hornets, McGuire Air Force Base, New Jersey...For flying an American flag in Jim's name over Afghanistan during Operation Enduring Freedom, having it signed by every member of your brave squadron, and sending it to me.

Thank you, Rich DePietro...For sculpting a small cross out of a steel girder from the World Trade Center and leaving it at my church for me. It is the only remembrance of Ground Zero that I cherish, and it was used as the basis of this book's cover.

Thank you, employees at the pharmacy...For contacting the United States Celestial Registry and dedicating a star in Jim's memory: Constellation Cetus, coordinates 2h 22m – 16.5 degrees. How cool is that! When I look up into the sky, I know that Jim is truly shining down on us.

E-mail message
From: Jim Sands
Sent: 12/14/00
To: Paul Barbaro
Subject: RE: eSpeed job offer

Hey Paul:
This seems like a really good opportunity to dig into a nice, juicy project together, and the potential upside looks really good from my point of view. Now is the right time to get a good strike price. The analysts love this company, and since it is public, we'll know FOR SURE at the end of the year whether we made the right decision or not. If I'm wrong, then I'm done forever with the Stock Options game, and I only lost one more year. Which is not the worst thing in the world.
Your thoughts?

Later—
Jim

Getting around on Crutches

16

Abraham Lincoln once wrote to a grieving family, "Sorrow comes to all...perfect relief is not possible, except with time. You cannot now realize that you will ever feel better...and yet you are sure to be happy again." No offense, Mr. Lincoln, but I must disagree with your theory that "perfect relief is not possible, except with time." Time does not heal all wounds. Some people die from wounds. Others just learn to live with the scars. Here's what I mean.

I read C.S. Lewis' book *A Grief Observed* about the loss of his wife. Lewis compares the loss of a loved one to an amputation of a limb. This is by far the closest analogy imaginable. After September 11th, I truly felt like I had lost a leg. After that sudden amputation, I had intense, fierce, continuous post-surgical pain. On the pain scale, it was a ten out of ten. In those early days, no sedatives or narcotics provided relief. I was faced with the concept of living the rest of my life without my leg. Without my husband.

Gradually, the stump began to heal, and it was no longer an open wound. I began to regain my strength, but I was limping around on one leg. I will always have recurrent pains in that stump forever. There will never be a moment when I will forget what was once there. Every detail in my life is now different and will continue to be for the rest of my life. Even the simplest things: driving, shopping, cooking, lying in bed. Things that I once enjoyed, I am no longer able to do, no longer interested in.

That's why they invented crutches, right? Of course, nothing — no one — will ever be a replacement for Jim. But crutches are necessary for survival. Without them, I'd be sitting in a wheelchair, totally dysfunctional. Many grieving people have chosen the wheelchair option. And it's a choice that presents itself: to sit while my mind and body deteriorate. To make myself and everyone around me miserable.

But there's another choice: to summon up all the strength I can and make the effort to walk. Take a few steps. Either hop on my good leg or use a crutch to make it a bit easier. For me, crutches saved my life. My crutches were my family, my friends, and my faith. Through them, I have learned how to get around. To get through this.

Will I ever find another man who can bring me so much happiness? Do I even want one? Do I even want to entertain the idea of one? What would be the odds of experiencing perfect love twice in one lifetime?

I have learned many things from this nightmare, and one of them is this: Few things in life are certain. The blinding truth of this doesn't hit home until something destroys every certainty you thought you had. Your happiness, your hopes, your dreams, your future, your best friend and soul mate. I will never be certain of anything again.

Uh oh, I feel another movie line coming. It's from *Men In Black*, when Tommy Lee Jones is talking to Will Smith about joining MIB to help regulate the disguised aliens living in our world. Jones says, "Five thousand years ago, everyone knew the earth was the center of the universe. Five hundred years ago, everyone knew that the earth was flat. And five minutes ago, you knew that humans were alone on this planet. Imagine what you'll know tomorrow."

Two years ago, I knew Jim and I would be together for the rest of our lives. Imagine what I'll know tomorrow.

Another man in my life? Right now, it's unthinkable. Right now, I believe the only way I would agree to it is if the guy fell out of the clouds and landed on my front porch with a sign around his neck that said, "Hi, Jim sent me." Even then, the poor guy would have to tolerate being constantly compared to Jim, the standard to whom all will be compared. If it's meant to be, it will be. I trust God with my future. With Him in my life, I will never be alone.

tf

Jim's on his first dive with an underwater camera. Both of us are low on air.

I signal to him, two thumbs pointed up: "Time to surface."

Jim writes on his dive slate: " I'm staying here forever. Keep sending down tanks!"

Jim Sands
Memorial Reef

17

Jim and I often traveled to Grand Cayman to dive, and over the years we became close friends with our dive instructor Elke, who lives on the island. It was a privilege to be trained by her, but even more of an honor to be her friend. The three of us would often dive together, then go out to dinner and truly enjoy each other's company. Elke always said that Jim was her "star pupil" because he was a "perfect diver" (of course, I agree).

About a week after September 11th, Elke came up with the idea to have a bronze plaque placed on one of Grand Cayman's coral reefs in Jim's memory. Her crusade was a difficult one that required negotiations with the Department of Environment. The Cayman Islands, a British protectorate, maintains some of the strictest marine preservation laws in the world. In March 2002, Elke finally gained permission from the Cayman government for the memorial plaque to be permanently mounted on a coral reef. The agreement required the plaque be made entirely from marine-friendly materials and its placement on the reef had to be on a sand patch so that no coral would be destroyed. No problem. We were set.

But in early April 2002 Elke told me that newly-elected government officials were taking office in two months, and she

Jim Sands Memorial Reef plaque.
Sculpted by Brian Hanlon.
Dedicated July, 2002.
Grand Cayman, British West Indies.

couldn't guarantee they would honor the previous administration's agreement. So a deadline ensued. The plaque must be in the water by June 1st.

I got busy. The bronze plaque was created here in New Jersey by talented artist/sculptor Brian Hanlon, who graciously agreed to put this project ahead of all others in order to make the deadline requirement, and he created a masterpiece in the process. As required, the plaque is made entirely of marine-friendly materials, and on it Brian sculpted Jim's face using photos I provided. The wording on the plaque reads: "In Memory of Jim Sands.... A Victim of the World Trade Center N.Y.C., September 11, 2001... Dive to Live, Live to Dive." The first time I saw the finished piece, I thought I was looking right into Jim's face and into his soul. Brian has a gift for sculpting, and as I've come to know him, a gift for friendship also.

The plaque was shipped to Grand Cayman in the second week of May. The island's Department of Environment chose the exact location for the plaque, which could not have been more perfect: a quiet, pristine reef just offshore from Cemetery Beach — one of the best shallow dives on the island. The plaque was permanently mounted under water in concrete at a depth of thirty feet on May 28th, 2002 — three days before the new government took office. Whew! A new mooring was built, and a new dive site was born. The site has been named by the island's dive operators as "Jim Sands Memorial Reef."

When Elke e-mailed to tell me the plaque had been mounted, I burst into tears. I felt the same way as when I read David Taylor's words that Jim's photos would be published in his favorite dive magazine. I felt that something very special had been done in his memory, and I was touched that so many people cared about him and wanted to pay tribute to him. Since none of Jim's remains were found, we had no cemetery or gravesite to visit and pay respects. I knew that I absolutely had to go visit the reef. That meant diving again. Without Jim. And that concept scared the heck out of me.

I planned the trip for a week in July 2002. I took along my sister Maria and her husband Tom. Tom had always wanted to learn how to dive, and I knew there could not be a better opportunity to be trained by the best — Elke.

I dreaded the trip. This was no vacation; it was a pilgrimage to a memorial. I knew this was an amazing tribute made possible by some very special people, but I also had anxiety about return-ing to the place where Jim and I had spent so much time, and where we planned to live one day. I expected to feel an even greater loss, because of all the memories we had made there.

Nothing could have been further from the truth. I felt Jim's presence more during that week than I had since the day he died. I know he was with me the entire time; I could actually feel it. And I came home with an inner peace that I did not have before.

The "Memorial Dive" was scheduled for Wednesday, July 17th. The weather was perfect, the water flat, and we had a private char-ter for the occasion. There were six of us on board: me, Maria (who does not dive), Tom (who had just become certified to dive the day before), Ryan (the boat captain), Carlin (the videographer — yes, this whole dive is on film), and Elke, her mission finally complete. I brought flowers to lay beside the plaque — five white calla lilies, our wedding flowers, one for each year we were married — and a conch shell to anchor them down under water. I brought the same photos of Jim that Brian had used to sculpt the plaque and displayed them on the boat. And I brought (and wore) Jim's favorite T-shirt, which announces his motto: "Dive to Live, Live to Dive." And then magical, unexplainable things began to happen. First was the "mysterious yellow raft incident."

My sister Maria is not a diver, a snorkeler, or even a good swimmer. She and her husband Tom have an inground pool at home, but Maria only uses it to float on her favorite yellow raft. It's common knowledge that anyone entering the pool should not touch Maria's raft — or else.

The day we arrived on Grand Cayman, the three of us walked down to the turquoise Caribbean outside our hotel. Maria said jokingly, "This is really paradise. The only thing missing is my raft."

Three days later, our boat was heading to Jim's reef for the memorial dive. We were quite a distance offshore with no other boats in sight, going full speed. Suddenly the boat captain cut the engines. As the boat slowed down, he squinted and said, "What's that up there?" We hustled to the front of the boat. "Look, there's something in the water."

As we drifted closer, we couldn't believe our eyes. It was Maria's yellow raft, identical to hers at home in every detail. It floated in front of our boat, fully inflated. Coincidence? Jim was well aware that Maria would be the only person on the boat that day who would not be able to see the plaque. He was making sure she could.

We pulled the raft aboard. Later, at the dive site, Maria donned mask and snorkel. Then, holding on for dear life to her yellow raft, which we had tied to the mooring buoy, she marveled at the beauty of the reef and Jim's plaque below, visible from above through Cayman's clear water. She later deflated the raft, brought it home, and wrote, "To Maria, with Love from Jim" on it to distinguish it from the original, which is identical.

97

As we neared Jim's reef that day, I began to imagine how proud Jim would be — no, how proud he is — to know that he had his very own site and a beautiful bronze plaque to welcome every diver who dives his reef. But I also began to worry about diving without the only dive buddy I'd ever had. I worried about seeing the plaque for the first time. I even worried about crying under water with a mask on my face and a regulator in my mouth.

We did our giant strides off the boat and headed down. Seeing the plaque for the first time was quite emotional. Tears quickly filled my mask, and I was constantly clearing it. Heavy sobs forced the regulator's exhaust bubbles out in erratic jets. It felt strange to cry while biting down on a mouthpiece. Yet I sensed Jim was there with me, admiring the plaque with his huge "I've got something you don't have" smirk on his face. And with that thought and image, the anxiety left me.

From that time on, the abundance of marine life was incredible. I have never seen so many different fish species on a single dive. Carlin was able to capture much of it on video, while Elke took still shots. I suddenly realized that virtually all the fish subjects that Jim had photographed — especially those that appeared in *Rodale's Scuba Diving* magazine — were presenting themselves in full glory: a curious barracuda hovered near us; a platter-shaped Queen Angel, resplendent in neon blue and yellow, swam shyly by; a giant spiny lobster waved antennae from a crevice; even a large hawksbill turtle uncharacteristically approached us and joined our party for a few minutes before paddling away. I felt as if Jim and I were exchanging gifts, as if he were acknowledging the publication of his photos.

98

But there was one toothy subject who showed up that Jim never had a chance to capture on film...the "mysterious sleeping shark."

Jim and I had an ongoing debate about sharks. Throughout

the four years we had been diving together, we had never seen a shark, and that was perfectly fine with him. I, on the other hand, have always wanted an up-close and personal shark encounter. Even though Jim knew that the shark's reputation was undeserved and based on Hollywood myth, he also admitted that he would be uncomfortable should he ever find himself in a shark's company. He would quote statistics about unprovoked shark attacks, and I would rebut that they were never on scuba divers. We had this conversation a hundred times, and Jim would always finish his case with: "The only way I'd ever be content seeing a shark is if it were sleeping."

After our silent memorial service at Jim's plaque, we began to swim around the newly dedicated "Jim Sands Memorial Reef." Elke, who was swimming slightly ahead of me, suddenly turned and raised her hand perpendicular to her forehead — a diver's hand signal for "shark." I froze. Then Elke placed her palms together and tilted her head to rest on them — the signal for an animal sleeping. Sure enough, as Elke moved us cautiously ahead, we saw a nurse shark snoozing in the sand under a coral ledge.

It was such a Jim-thing to do: another gift, but this one on his terms — a shark that was out like a light. Even then, he was still protecting me. And getting the last word.

Tom did great on his first dive as a fully certified diver and even provided comic relief on the video with his acrobatics. Except for his mask, he was wearing all of Jim's scuba equipment, and I'm sure that made Jim happy. Tom always told Jim, "When you become an instructor, I'll be your first student." Tom has now fallen in love with this sport, and yet another dive monster has been created.

So what started out as anxiety ended up as comfort and peace. This has become Jim's true final resting place, and he made sure I knew he was happy about that. I know there will always be a part of him in Grand Cayman. Never could I have imagined that I would want to return there, but now I can't wait to make a yearly pilgrimage to visit the "Jim Sands Memorial Reef".

It gives me something to look forward to.

I set my tea mug down on the kitchen countertop and...crunch, my mug grinds into the sugar scattered all over the place. I hate that sound, it sends chills down my spine. Jim must have refilled the sugar bowl again. He always manages to miss the sugar bowl as he pours from the five-pound bag.

"Hey, you got sugar all over the counter again!" I yell to him in the next room.

He sighs so loud I can hear it. "Okay, fine. From now on, I'll let you fill up the sugar bowl."

"Fine with me! At least I'm careful about it."

A week later — 4:45 A.M. I'm sound asleep. Jim nudges my arm. I open my eyes and there he is — sugar bowl in one hand, big bag of sugar in the other, and a triumphant look in his eyes.

"Hon, the sugar bowl's empty," he says.

The Two-Headed
Guilt Monster

18

Ladies and Gentlemen, allow me to introduce the "two-headed guilt monster." One head delivers a toxic dose of blame for my past cruelties to Jim. The other head stings me with the venom of shame when I experience any joy in my new life.

Confession time: I did some things I'm not proud of during our marriage. No mortal sins, no grounds for divorce, just things that eat away at me and make me feel ashamed of myself. I don't think I sacrificed nearly as much for Jim as he sacrificed for me. He gave away his beloved premarital cat Tigger upon my insistence. (I was allergic, and I'm not a cat lover.) He sold his beloved premarital Corvette and Sea Ray boat upon my persuasion. (I contended they were costly and impractical.) I refused to allow him to have his own comfortable recliner in our newly renovated family room. ("Sorry, hon, but a La-Z-Boy just will not blend with the décor.") The poor guy had less closet space than Stuart Little, while I hoarded the entire walk-in closet to myself.

Although I know we had a loving, happy marriage, I can't help kicking myself that there were things I could have done to make it even happier for him. Any therapist would say that if Jim were here right now, he would be quick to point out all the times that I compromised for him. But Jim isn't here, and my own sacrifices don't seem to mean much anymore. And so, I find myself succumbing to the evil force of the guilt monster: Would it have been the end of the world if a big, overstuffed, mismatched recliner ruined the aesthetics of a room? Would it have killed me to create space in my closet for some of his clothes? How much happier would he have been had he spent the last years of his life enjoying his cat, his sports car, and his boat? It's amazing how trivial his requests seem now; at the time, it was critically important for the spoiled brat to get her way.

I'm anxiously awaiting the day when a time machine will be invented. I'll gladly be the first volunteer for a test run. Knowing what I know now, at what point in my past would I set the time? Would I go back to the morning of September 11th and create a physical blockade so Jim couldn't leave the house? Would I go back farther, to the early years of our marriage, so I could "fix" the things I did wrong by allowing the cat to stay and simply taking Benadryl when my allergies acted up? Might I even consider going back to our first date and, knowing what I know now, change the course of events by never accepting a second date? Is it really "better to have loved and lost, than never to have loved at all"?

Sometimes, when the pain becomes unbearable, there's a part of me that wishes I had never met Jim; then I'd be spared the suffering. It's selfish, I know. Certainly I am a much better person in every way for knowing him and loving him and instantly bonding with him. But those feelings of being "gypped" still inhabit my mind. Imagine you're homeless and destitute. You pray every day for your life to dramatically change for the better. Then one day, someone gives you a lottery ticket and...Yee-hah! Your numbers are drawn, and you win the multi-million-dollar tri-state jackpot! So, for over six years, you enjoy the wealth and riches in ways that you once only dreamed of. Life is beautiful.

But then one day comes a knock on the door. It's an official lottery agent with the bad news: "We regret to inform you that there was an error. You really did not win; it was all a big mistake. We're truly sorry, but you must return all the money that you have not yet spent. We'll let you keep the memories you've already made. But we must take back the remainder of the prize." My life was empty before I met Jim. Then I met him, and I felt like I had truly won the "love and happiness jackpot." Now the emptiness is even greater, because now I've been robbed of a dream that came true.

So at one end of the spectrum is the Black Hole. At the other end is the two-headed guilt monster. They are opposing forces, and sometimes I feel like the ball in a game of emotional Ping-Pong. If I sit and sulk and brood over my sorrow and become bitter, angry, depressed, despondent, and miserable to be around, I will distance my family and friends — and get way too close to the edge of the Black Hole. Whoa, back off, as far away as possible. I imagine Cher standing in front of me. She slaps me across the face and yells, "Snap out of it!" (*Moonstruck*). So I shift gears and head over in the other direction. I take a deep breath and smile and go about my new life as normally as I possibly can with my spirit uplifted. But uh-oh, here comes that guilt monster again: "What right do you have to be happy?" it demands to know.

Is there a direct correlation between how much I love Jim and how upset I should be that he died? If the intensity of my grief is related to the intensity of my love for him, then shouldn't I be institutionalized by now? Okay, guilt monster, let's have it. How can a young widow laugh and not feel ashamed? If I don't continually express my grief and sadness, then how will Jim know, as he watches me from above, the extent of how much I truly love him and miss him?

My answer to the monster: Because soul mates just know. They don't need proof. One already knows how the other thinks. Soul mates know us better than we know ourselves. I love Jim more than any words can ever express, and he knows that. And his love for me is still flaming in my heart. Jim is a part of me, forever. I must, therefore, look for ways to honor him, to keep his memory alive. To be not only his "surviving spouse," but his "surviving spirit." As the rose left without a Lenox vase, it is my responsibility. It is the reason I'm writing this.

Finding that emotional balance isn't easy. So far, I've been fortunate to find it a few times: when Jim's underwater photos were published and when the bronze memorial plaque was placed on a reef in Cayman. These very special tributes allowed me to once again experience happiness, knowing that I did something that Jim would be proud of. And I did them without fat, calories, narcotics, or guilt.

·Ⅎf·

I'm folding laundry. Jim comes flying up to me clutching the manuscript of a monthly medical column I write for the local paper. "Hon, you can't say this!" His face is dead serious.

"Say what?"

"You can't call the article 'Jewish Penicillin.' It's not politically correct!"

"It's about the medicinal benefits of chicken soup," I say. "Hebrews will be flattered."

"Not a wise move, hon, somebody's gonna get pissed off."

He could be right. He usually is. "Okay," I say. "Think of another title, and if I like it, I'll use it."

An hour later he's back. "Got it?" I ask.

"Got it."

"So, let's hear it."

"Chickacillin."

And so it was.

Condolences:
Round Two

19

Returning to work
after September 11th was inevitable. I needed the money. The
generous financial support from the various September 11th
agencies, which literally saved me from losing my home and my
car, was slowing down. I will be forever grateful for this support,
but I also knew that if I didn't look ahead, I would soon be in
dangerous economic territory.

My boss and friend Rich needed help at the pharmacy, although he graciously told me to return only when I was ready. I
had been working for Rich since graduating from pharmacy
school in 1989. Ours is not the typical employer/employee relationship. Rich and I have journeyed together through tough
times over the years, and I cherish his wisdom and friendship.
Together we've been through divorces, weddings, births, deaths,
surgeries, and everything in between. We celebrated my happiness when I met and married Jim; we celebrated his happiness
when he met and married his wife, Lisa. Together, the four of us
were the closest of friends. And then there were three.

I also felt the pull of our customers. Many come from several
large senior citizen housing developments close to the store.
These people trust us for their health needs, for delivery service,
and for peace of mind. In many instances, our customers have

become like family; some visit us more often than their grown children visit them. Having worked there for thirteen years, I've become close to many of them. They've been with me through the happiest times of my life — my graduation, the purchase of my home, and my marriage — and now, they were going to be with me through the darkest days of my life. These loyal customers and friends needed to see me in the store again.

And so it began — round two of accepting condolences. But this was worse than the crowd of six hundred people at Jim's memorial service. This was a continual, daily presence of well-meaning customers who simply wanted to give me a hug and tell me how sorry they were. Kind gestures, indeed. But remember pharmacists work in a fishbowl. Pharmacy is the only profession I know of where someone making life-critical decisions is on display to the public, a public that is allowed to interrupt this professional at any time. Can you imagine family members being allowed in an operating room, then asking the surgeon just before he makes a critical incision, "Excuse me, doc, but is this going to take long?"

When I first went back to work, it took every ounce of energy to focus on my job. If I were filling prescriptions in a locked room with no windows and no distractions whatsoever, it still would have been miraculous that no mistakes were made during a complex process that few people comprehend. The public generally believes that a pharmacist simply dumps pills from a big bottle into a little bottle. In reality, each prescription goes through multiple checks: we confirm that the strength and dosage of the medication is appropriate for that drug. We verify that the strength and dosage of the medication is appropriate for the age and weight of the patient. We ensure that the patient is not taking any other medication that would adversely interact with it. We confirm that the correct stock bottle gets pulled out of inventory, is accurately counted or measured, and is placed in the correct patient's bottle. We must make sure that everything printed on the patient's label is correct. One slip of the finger on the keyboard and you might type "QID" instead of "QD." Translation: four times daily, instead of once daily.

But when our customers discovered the curly-haired goldfish was back, swimming around behind the counter in the pharmacy fish bowl, they wanted to acknowledge my loss. Many of them brought me cards, cookies, and gifts, and their genuine concern for me was truly appreciated. Most of them realized that I probably didn't want to talk about it, especially while I was filling their prescriptions. So they would simply walk past the counter and say, "I just want to let you know you are in my prayers, and I'm really glad to see you back."

Thank you for your prayers, and thank you for keeping it short.

But others could not contain themselves. Out of obligation, or the need for their own emotional release, or the need to comfort me, or their desire to help me, or a combination of all that and more, they insisted on expressing their concern face-to-face: "Oh, Jennifer, it's so good to see you. I've been thinking of you so much. Can I please give you a hug?"

And what could I possibly say: "No, sorry. I'm busy. I can't come out there to accept your sincere words of sympathy. Thanks, anyway." So, I would stop what I was doing, go out to dear Mrs. Jones who, as soon as she saw me, would burst into tears. (I think I became the community symbol for the nation's terrorist tragedy, because everyone who saw me had the same reaction.) Of course, when Mrs. Jones began crying, I would too, and pretty soon everyone standing within twenty feet of us was crying. Then came the worst part: I had to go back to what I was doing before I was called away.

Okay, take a deep breath. Stop thinking about the graphic comment that Mrs. Jones made about how bodies are still being found. Let's see, where was I...oh yeah, trying to figure out this dose of Coumadin. Wait, better blow my nose first.

This continued on a regular basis for quite some time. Fortunately, there was always another pharmacist who continuously checked my work. Some days I was especially sensitive. And some days there were a few insensitive customers. I tried so hard to maintain some degree of professional integrity, but certain comments and questions completely blew me away. An instant meltdown would follow, and I'd leave skid marks on the way to the ladies room.

Like the day old Mr. Smith yelled (he's hard of hearing) from the register, "DID THEY FIND YOUR HUSBAND'S BODY YET?"

Or the day that Mrs. Miller looked at me and said, "What you need is a nice, young man."

Or the day Mrs. White said, "How do you think I feel? I've buried *two* husbands already!"

Or the day Mr. Bell said, "Oh, he worked for Cantor? That's a shame. I heard those guys were trapped alive for over an hour."

Or the day Mrs. Milano asked, "Did he call you from the burning towers that morning?" I shook my head no. "That's too bad," she continued. "A lot of women heard from their husbands, and at least they got to say goodbye to each other."

I wanted to say that, if I had the choice between getting a frantic phone call from Jim after the towers were hit — and therefore knowing he was alive when the towers collapsed — or not getting a phone call — and allowing myself to believe it was because he had already perished quickly and painlessly — which do you think I'd choose? Jim and I said our goodbyes that morning. And I will forever be grateful that his final words to me

112

were, "I love you," instead of "Hon, the smoke is so thick I can hardly breathe."

The customer names have been changed, of course, and I know they never intentionally meant to upset me. Most of them never even knew they did, because I quickly and diplomatically excused myself before the volcanic eruption of tears. Truth is, there is very little one can say to make someone in my position feel better. But there's a heck of a lot one can say to make the grieving person feel worse. It's human nature for people to assume that they have to say something and that it would be worse to not speak at all.

My recommendation is to make a simple, sincere comment: "I'm sorry for your loss. Let me know if there's anything I can do." For me those are the safest and most comforting words.

Going back to work was physically, mentally, and emotionally exhausting. Many of my co-workers have since learned to recognize when it is necessary to run interference with certain customers. They have done an outstanding job of protecting me from potential meltdown hazards, and much of the initial strain has subsided. My biggest fear on the job is making a critical mistake and hurting someone. On a bad day, believe me, you do not want me filling your prescription. Rich has been extremely cooperative and flexible with my schedule, and on those "bad" days, he knows it is better for everyone involved if I just stay home.

In retrospect, it was wise to return to work. I could have chosen to depend financially on the Red Cross for at least one year. I could have told Rich, "Sorry, but you'll have to find a replacement." It would have been easier to sit home all day, every day, until the Black Hole engulfed me. Sadly, many grieving people chose that option. But thanks to encouraging words and endless support from my family, friends, co-workers, customers, and especially Rich, I have conquered the battle of the drugstore condolences — and won.

·ʄ·

"I could be wrong. It's been known to happen from time to time."

~Jim Sands

Witness for
the Defense

20

Of course not all of the "sympathy incidents" came from pharmacy customers. When I talk to unfamiliar people about losing my husband on September 11th, it invariably provokes the same questions:

"How long were you guys married?" *Five years.* "Oh, well that's good. At least it wasn't too long. It would be worse if you were married like, twenty years or something. You're still young. You'll get over it."

"Do you have any children?" *No.* "Oh, that's a good thing. At least you only have to take care of yourself. That must make your life much easier."

"How is Cantor treating you?" *Fine. They've been wonderful, very supportive to the families.* "That's good to hear, because I heard you guys really got screwed." *On the contrary. They've gone the extra mile for us.*

I am always quick to smother any leftover bad publicity that Howard Lutnick, the company's CEO, had once unfairly received. Soon after the attack, Cantor Fitzgerald announced that the company would remove the victims from the payroll. The last paycheck we would receive would be September 15, 2001. This outraged several of the widows and surviving family members, who banded together and appeared on national television berating the company and its CEO: "What are we supposed to do? We have children to support; we have bills to pay." They blamed Howard Lutnick for callously terminating their income. They also complained about how poorly Cantor communicated with the victims' families in the early days after the attack.

They failed to consider an important fact: Cantor Fitzgerald, along with its subsidiaries eSpeed and TradeSpark, was gone. Destroyed. The companies no longer existed. Where did these women think the salaries were going to come from? It never crossed my mind that I would continue to receive Jim's paychecks. I completely understood the financial strain these families were under — I was in the same boat. But I didn't understand why they felt they were entitled to paychecks from companies that had been wiped out. As far as the lack of communication in the days after September 11th — there were 657 Cantor employees killed that day. Exactly who was left to answer the phones and handle the questions?

The critics also did not think, for just a moment, what Howard Lutnick must have been going through. In an instant of madness, he lost his company and all of his employees, including his own brother. By an unfathomable quirk of fate — he was dropping his son off at his first day of kindergarten — Lutnick wasn't in his office that morning to perish with the rest. In those first days after the tragedy, Howard was in no position, emotionally or financially, to address the concerns of these grieving widows. Yet they blamed him anyway, as if Howard were somehow responsible for the disaster and should therefore also be responsible for keeping the money coming.

118   Although Howard Lutnick was under no obligation to take care of the Cantor families, he has since made it his mission to do so. He established the Cantor Fitzgerald Relief Fund, which provides ongoing financial assistance to the families. He has

promised to pay our health insurance for ten years. He has become our advocate in the many issues that we encounter as families of the victims. He has gone above and beyond the call of his duty, and thankfully, the public criticism has eased considerably. So, on behalf of your "new" family, thank you, Howard, for choosing to give us something to look forward to.

As long as I'm on the defense bandwagon, I feel the need to assure everyone reading this that if you were one of the countless people who made a donation to the American Red Cross for 9/11 disaster relief, your money did indeed pull us out of dire straits. The Red Cross was also the prey of negative publicity. Allegations were made that families were not receiving the money required to meet their daily needs. On the contrary, the Red Cross not only financially supported me until I could get back on my feet, (and I know for a fact this holds true for every family affected by the September 11th events), but their volunteers were some of the kindest and most compassionate people I have ever encountered.

When I went to obtain Jim's death certificate in Jersey City, where trailers had been set up for disaster relief, a Red Cross volunteer was assigned to me. This angel never left my side for a single second throughout a long and traumatic day. She held my hand, she cried with me, and she walked with me from trailer to trailer. She was my voice that day, my strength and my shoulder to cry on. She promised me that everything would be okay, even though she knew I could not fathom that at the time. I never saw her again after that day. But I can still picture her face, and I remember her name. Christine Moulon, wherever you are, I thank you from the bottom of my heart for keeping me out of the Black Hole that day. You were — and are — an inspiration to me. Because of you, I am considering joining the Red Cross and dedicating my life to helping victims of other disasters. tf

119

Shopping in a leather store, Jim is hunting for a new briefcase. Like every-thing else he buys, it's a major production. No matter what the purchase — from a ballpoint pen to new golf clubs — Jim analyzes, considers, recon-siders, picks up, puts down, over and over for hours.

"No such thing as a quick decision for you, is there?" I ask.

"They just don't make what I want." He's annoyed that the briefcase with the better compartments only comes in brown, not black.

"Such a dilemma." I'm patronizing him now. "And the more choices you have, the more you struggle to choose."

"Not always." He grins. "The biggest decision I ever made was also the easiest. I picked you. It was a no-brainer."

The First
Christmas

21

To say that I am
a completely different person than I was before Jim died is an
understatement. There have been so many changes in my life —
mental, emotional, spiritual, physical — and I'm sure more are
coming. So far I can identify myself as three distinct and consec-
utive individuals: the person I was before September 11th, the
person I was for about four months after Jim died, and the person I have slowly transformed into today. But the time in between still makes me cringe.

The first year without your loved one lives up to its reputation as the most difficult. Every birthday, holiday, and anniversary is a reality brick. Each one forces you to remember happy
memories of past birthdays, holidays, and anniversaries that will
never be celebrated the same again. I also involuntarily began
counting the days since September 11th. Every dreaded morning
when I wake up, my mind automatically adds *one* to the number
from the day before.

This subconscious math started the day after the tragedy and
has continued ever since. Today is Day 522. I do not write it
down, I have never calculated it out. I just know that yesterday
was Day 521. I can still remember how I felt on certain days. For
instance, I remember Day 17 — the day of Jim's Memorial Mass.

I remember Day 100, because of the pointless significance of hitting triple digits. I remember Day 366 (September 11, 2002) because I felt the same way that I felt on Day 1.

Day 106: My first Christmas without Jim. Somehow, celebrating the birth of our Savior did not seem very important compared to what I had lost. But, amazingly, I did receive a big surprise: an actual Christmas present from Jim.

It was Christmas Eve, 2001. I had made an agreement with my family to keep gifts to a bare minimum. I went into the attic to find wrapping paper for the few small gifts I had bought for my nine-year-old niece, Tarah. The search for Christmas wrap involved moving boxes and luggage and old computer equipment and — *What's in this black plastic bag? Hmmm, it doesn't look familiar.* I opened it up. And there, inside, was a wrapped Christmas present.

I realized instantly what had happened. At some unknown point in the past, Jim had bought me something for Christmas, wrapped it, and hid it in the attic amongst his computer equipment, knowing I'd never find it. Then he completely forgot about it. Who knows how long it had been there, buried behind old monitors and keyboards.

I sat on top of a suitcase, took a deep breath, and opened Jim's Christmas present. It was a ceramic Christmas village house from the collectibles made by Department 56. I collect the "Christmas in the City" set, and Jim had picked out one that I had always wanted: The Arts Academy, which had since been retired. So, there I was, sitting in a dim attic, sobbing uncontrollably. Part of me cried because I wished so badly for him to be sitting next to me as I unwrapped it. Part of me cried because I believed he had guided me through the attic, so I would discover the forgotten present. Jim made sure he gave me a Christmas present that year. Today I keep The Arts Academy displayed all year long, cherishing it with all my heart.

Thanks, hon...I love you too.

By the time our birthdays rolled around in April and May, I was emotionally stronger, less angry, less bitter. I had progressed from having "bad days and worse days" to having "bad days and good days." For our wedding anniversary on May 4, 2002, I racked up all the courage I could and watched our wedding video by myself. I cried through most of it, but I also found comfort in the memories. At this time, I was emerging from these dark days into a new chapter of my life where I could think of Jim and talk about him freely without going into a downward spiral. In July 2002, the possibility of the bronze memorial plaque became a reality. The trip to Cayman and Jim's reef brought me a new level of inner peace. I was feeling so much stronger.

Then came a new and unwelcome anniversary: September 11, 2002.

·tf·

Jim is giving me the lowdown on his new job at eSpeed. I've never been inside the World Trade Center, and I can't imagine working so close to the top of a skyscraper.

"There's so much sway in the building," Jim says, "it's going to take some getting used to."

"Sway? Really? You feel it?"

"Feel it and see it. The guys in the office hang their computer mouses from the ceiling and watch them swing. I feel like I'm on a boat."

"That's wild."

"When you go into the men's room, the water in the toilet swishes from side to side."

My eyes keep getting bigger. "When you look outside your office window, can you see cars and people?"

"Outside my window? Hon, when I look outside my window, I see clouds! We're inside the clouds!"

Then he adds, "But the strangest thing is when planes fly by. They're so close to us and so loud, the whole building resonates with the sound and shakes. It's freaky."

September 11, 2002: A Day at Ground Zero

21

Until September, the first year of special occasions without Jim involved reminders of good times, albeit painful ones to recall. But this occasion was different. It was the anniversary of our darkest hours.

As the day approached, I forced myself to confront what my plans would be, to decide where and how I would spend that day. I knew two things for sure:

I did not want to be alone.

I did not want to be home. It is where we held vigil last year on 9/11 in front of the wide-screen TV, and I didn't want to be reminded of that scenario.

Throughout the year, I had no desire to visit Ground Zero. I knew I wasn't emotionally ready. Many families of the WTC victims would make frequent visits to the site, apparently finding some inner peace or closure there. Many of them watched as recovery efforts took place and the cleanup ensued. Perhaps they felt a responsibility to their loved ones. Perhaps they experienced the presence of their loved ones on this sacred ground. Perhaps they were still holding on with a grip so tight that it could not be broken. I simply wanted to avoid the biggest reality brick of all time.

But when faced with the question of where I would be on the

one-year anniversary of my husband's death, it occurred to me that if I were ever going to make a trip to Ground Zero, this would be the time. My family and I drove up to New York on the night of September 10th, where we met with Jim's family to stay in a hotel overnight. Since thousands of people were expected to gather at 7:00 A.M. for the planned ceremonies, it would be easier to already be in the city instead of driving in at that hour. In the room that night with my mom and sister Maria, I wanted nothing more than to leave. But then I felt an obligation to Jim to make an attempt at the very least. I prayed to God to get me through the day.

Walking the few blocks from our hotel to Ground Zero was terrifying. Thousands of people moved in a crowd together, yet everything was deathly quiet. Ahead of us was the entrance to the site. I began to visibly tremble as we approached it. The memory of how I felt that morning, one year ago, when I turned on the TV — the feeling in the pit of my stomach, the weakness, the racing heart — all came flooding back when I looked at the colossal hole in the ground. Then suddenly the words that raced through my head with every breath one year before came rushing back:

This can't be happening.

And yet here I was at Ground Zero, and before me was this undeniable reality that it *had* happened and that it was worse than I dared to imagine.

126

After several security checks and gridlocked lines of people, we finally reached the area where the names of the victims would be read. Everyone packed tightly together, sharing a common bond and waiting for the ceremonies to begin at 8:30 A.M. As the bagpipes and drum processionals marched closer to the site, my body shook harder and my heart beat faster. Amazing how bagpipes have that effect.

We stood in place, packed like sardines for over four hours, while we listened to the moments of silence and tolling of bells (one at 8:46 A.M. when the first plane hit the North Tower and one at 10:29 A.M. when the North Tower collapsed), then the reading of each name of the 2,823 people killed that day. I held my breath in anticipation when they reached the Ss...then it finally came over the loudspeaker: "James Sands, Jr."

Huddled with my family and Jim's, we clutched each other's hands and cried. Hearing his name was a giant reality brick for all of us.

For the first time, the families were allowed to descend the ramp into the seven-story pit to mourn on sacred ground. We decided we would go. After all, we'd come this far, might as well go all the way. Every person descending into The Pit was given a rose to place at the circle, and we had brought photos of Jim to leave there as well.

As I walked down the ramp, the enormity of this disaster struck me once again. The Pit had been cleaned up as much as possible over the past year, but to me, it still looked ugly and raw, like an open wound. It was devastating to look at. I couldn't imagine how horrible it must have looked one year ago. I couldn't believe my Jim was killed right here on this spot. All I saw was ruins — of the towers and of our lives. I couldn't wait to leave.

Anyone who watched the coverage of this event on television will remember how windy it was at Ground Zero that day. Forceful gusts blew the dirt around like mini-twisters. It was downright spooky. Our clothes quickly became soiled, our faces developed a layer of visible gray dust, and it became difficult to breathe. We were reminders of the ash-covered apparitions that

127

America watched fleeing for their lives one year before. Yet we were standing still and silent, gray ghosts of the dead.

The President and First Lady arrived in The Pit for a wreath-laying ceremony and to greet the families. I remember thinking that, under any other circumstances, I would be excited to meet the President. But standing in the middle of The Pit, in the footprints of the towers, marking the last moments of my husband's life, all I could think about was leaving — as soon as possible.

I made my request known to my family, and we headed for the ramp but were stopped by one of a thousand Secret Service agents, who informed us that for security reasons we were not permitted to exit The Pit until the President and First Lady themselves had left.

We were trapped. Once again, I was forced to imagine what it must have been like to be trapped alive in those burning towers with every exit blocked.

It was two hours before the President finished the handshakes and made his way back up the ramp. I couldn't leave the city fast enough, and I was never so happy to be home again. Physically, I was exhausted and filthy. My clothes were black; there was dirt in my ears, my eyes, my nose; and it coated every uncovered area of my body. Mentally, I was spent. I personally did not find peace there, although many people do. For me, it was an overdose of reality. It was blatant proof of how Jim died, not of how he lived, and that went against my preference of how I choose to remember him.

Before leaving for New York, people attempted to encourage me by saying, "Oh, I'm sure Jim will be there with you in spirit." And I would reply, "But why would he — or his spirit — ever want to go back there?" Perhaps he did show up to see us. But I wouldn't blame him a bit if he didn't. One thing is for sure: I shan't be returning there any time soon.

September 11, 2002: A Day at Ground Zero

The good news is, when it was all over, I did feel a sense of relief. The next day seemed slightly different than any other day in the past year. Again, I had forced myself to face the pain instead of hiding from it, and I was better for doing that. The 9/11 anniversary of Jim's death was also the last of the firsts without Jim, so there were no more calendar hurdles to dread. Those special occasions will always be difficult. But getting the "firsts" out of the way lightened the burden. I also felt a sense of accomplishment. I got through my first year without him.

One down...

I'm making dinner as Jim walks in the door, exhausted from another long day.

"Hi, hon." He drops his briefcase on the floor and comes over to give me a kiss.

Here it comes. He's about to do his after-work comedy routine. Sure enough —

"I'm a shell of a man," he starts, trying to look and sound like Kramer from Seinfeld. "I'm fallin' apart. I got stomach problems, sinus problems, carpel tunnel syndrome, chronic headaches, every muscle in my body hurts."

That's my usual cue in this family skit. "I know, hon, you're just a mess."

"I need a new life..." he mumbles, shaking his head in disgust.

"Oh? Can I be a part of it?" I try to be as sarcastic as possible.

"Duh, of course, hon!" He rolls his eyes and waves his arms. "But at this rate, I'm not gonna make it to the age of forty. I'm a shell of a man, Jerry!"

Crying with Hope

23

This chapter's title is taken from a Steven Curtis Chapman song, "With Hope." Chapman says that we can cry with hope, grieve with hope, and even say goodbye with hope because we will see that person again in heaven. Chapman's song puts into words what is in my heart right now.

Never could I have imagined that I would lose the love of my life so early in our marriage in a global tragedy.

Never could I have imagined that this disaster would really not be the end of me, and that I would one day be functional again.

Never could I have imagined that scuba diving would introduce me not only to the underwater world but to another world as well: a world of new friends whose tributes to Jim after his death not only honored him but rescued me.

Never could I have imagined that I would write a book. A book. It still doesn't seem possible. But sometimes none of this seems possible.

But it did happen. It all happened. September 11th happened. Meltdowns. Reality bricks. Black holes. Jim's photos published. A coral reef and a bronze plaque dedicated to him in a foreign country. And a book, which I hope is proof that the spirit of our loved ones and of our nation can truly survive even the darkest moments of disaster.

Which brings me back to my obsession with counting the days since September 11th. Since I can't seem to break the habit, I have given it a different twist. I still wake up every morning and add *one* to the number from the day before. But now, in addition to thinking *It's been 522 days since I saw Jim*, I attach:

And one day closer to seeing him again.

As I look back on that first year, I realize God has placed certain people in my life — like Elke and Willem and Ethel and David and Teresa — for reasons that are now clear to me. God has strategically orchestrated my life and provided people who have become instrumental in my healing. Friends who started out as strangers, who live thousands of miles away from me, some of whom I've never met — these people have helped me through the most difficult times of my life.

Every family of the September 11th victims has a story to tell. Stories of the happy lives they shared with their loved ones and the horrific details of that fateful day. We have all made a journey, and we will continue on this journey forever. There will never be complete closure. There will never be an end to the grief. But the strength and passion of this country — and of the families who live on as ambassadors of the ones we loved — these will always endure.

No, we cannot and will not forget them. Their spirit survives in every one of us.

Crying with Hope

> *For I know the plans I have for you...to give you hope and a future.*
>
> ~Jeremiah 29:11 (NIV)

tf

I believe in the sun, even when it is not shining...
I believe in hope, even when I have none...
I believe in love, even when it is taken from me...
I believe in God, even though I cannot see His face.

~Written on a wall in the Warsaw Ghetto in 1939, by an
11-year old girl being led away to the camps.

A 9/11
Diary

24

In December 2001, my nephew Kevin gave me a very special Christmas gift: *Grace for the Moment Journal*, Max Lucado's daily devotional prayer journal. On each day's page is a passage of Scripture and a writing prompt from Lucado based on that Scripture. I wrote in this journal daily during 2002. Little did I know the role it would play in my life and in the writing of this book. Little did I know that it would be a daily record of the long journey I took in 2002 from a faith challenged to a faith confirmed, from weakness and despair to strength and resolve.

These entries are my conversations with God. They are my pleas to Him for wisdom and understanding. They reveal the struggles of my life, and my struggle to trust Him.

They are my prayers.

January 1, 2002

> *God wants to hear what you have to say. How does that make you feel?**

It makes me wonder why I even bother praying, since You're just gonna do whatever You want anyway...Well, I might as well start

---

*All quoted material is reprinted from Max Lucado's *Grace for the Moment Journal* with permission.

out the year with a resolution to write to You every night. Just in case you really are listening.

January 2, 2002

I have another resolution: I swear, right now, that I will NEVER, EVER again say, "things have to get better, 'cause they can't get any worse." Jim and I both said that, exactly one year ago today. Guess we were wrong, big time.

January 4, 2002

> *God loves to decorate...this might explain some of the discomfort in your life. Remodeling of the heart is not always pleasant. We don't object when the Carpenter adds a few shelves, but He's been known to gut the entire west wing...He won't stop until He is finished.... He wants you to be just like Jesus.*

Not a good day. Multiple technological crises. Power failure. Computer problems. You know how paranoid I am about Jim's computers. Tonight is the Comcast e-mail transition at midnight. I'm predicting big problems, since I don't know Jim's password. Am I supposed to cast *this* anxiety onto You too? Fine. Then give me Jim's password and take a break from remodeling.

January 5, 2002

Today I stumbled upon Jim's Bible. I didn't even know he owned one. And inside, (tucked in the gospel of Luke), was a piece of scrap paper with Marc's phone number written in Jim's handwriting. Since Marc knows how Jim networked his computers, I suppose You think it would be a good idea for me to call Marc for help with the password and the e-mail problems. Okay.

A 9/11 Diary

January 7, 2002
I still can't sleep at night. I see Jim's face, constantly, in my mind. How am I going to live the rest of my life without him? Why did this happen to us, Lord? Why did you *let* this happen?

January 8, 2002
I thought we had an "understanding," Lord: I believe in You, so when I ask You for things, You give them to me. That's how we always worked it, remember? This feels like a breach of contract. Or at least a breach of etiquette. I feel violated. I am so lost without him, Lord.

January 9, 2002
I found a greeting card in Jim's desk drawer — one that he had bought for me but never gave to me. Inside, it said: "You. Me. Eternity." Is this a promise, Lord? Please don't let me down on that one.

January 11, 2002
I just cannot believe that four months ago, my life changed forever. It still does not seem possible. And no matter how hard I try, I cannot — and will not — ever have the answers I am looking for. Why, Lord? Why? Why do things have to be this way? And how am I going to live without him? I am not strong enough for this.

January 13, 2002
Went to church for the first time since 9/9/01, as You know. Could not stop thinking about all that went on there. I look at the altar and see Jim and I on our wedding day. Then I see us sitting in our usual seats every Sunday for Mass. Then I see the altar filled with flowers and the portrait of Jim at his Memorial

Mass. It really hurts to be there. I sure hope You appreciate that I actually went.

January 14, 2002
We spent the day with Anthony today. His hair is starting to grow in again, since the radiation treatments are over. His faith in You has never faltered, though he has endured so much suffering. He gives You all the credit. I guess he's right. He's beaten all the odds and baffled the medical field, that's for sure. Thank You for helping my brother.

January 16, 2002

> *Though you hear nothing, He is speaking. Though you see nothing, He is acting. With God, there are no accidents. Every incident is intended to bring us closer to Him.*

I guess I can find some comfort in this. I suppose You know what You're doing. I do feel closer to You, but couldn't You have found some other way of making that happen?

January 17, 2002
Someone gave me a book today: *Healing Grief.* Started reading it, but once I realized it was about psychic powers, I lost interest and it lost credibility. The thing that bothered me the most was that it described You as a "term for love." What's that about? You're not a *term* or a *concept*, like something in a dictionary. You're a true Being and Spirit — and You are my Creator. I'm still trying to figure out this mess You've gotten me into, but I know You're going to explain it all to me one day.

138

January 19, 2002

Today was supposed to be our yearly "Day in New York," when Rich and Lisa and Jim and I take a limo and go to dinner and a show in the city. We've had tickets since last summer to see *The Producers* today. Jim was really looking forward to this one. My heart is breaking. Instead, my nephew Brian came over, and we watched a few movies and ate tons of junk food. Thanks, Lord, for giving us an enjoyable time together.

January 20, 2002

Here is one of my struggles, Lord: How do I know the difference between Your will and free will? You gave us free will. And we exercise it often. Was 9/11 the result of a madman's free will? Or YOUR will? Whose plan was this? If You knew about it and allowed it anyway, then was it Your will or free will? Can't wait to hear the punch line, Lord.

January 23, 2002

I actually don't mind spending this quiet time writing to You every night before I go to bed. Much better than those nights of screaming and cursing at you, huh? I'm sorry I was so angry with You. Thanks for not being angry back at me. Just promise me you'll explain all of this one day.

January 24, 2002

Big day today! Got the magazines with Jim's photos and David's story! I saw the preview last month, but this is the real thing. Lord, please bless David Taylor and everyone at Rodale for doing this. I made a wish and held my breath, and David simply granted that wish — and made Jim's dream come true. Lord, please make sure Jim knows about this...he'll be so thrilled. The

139

only thing that could top this would be to see Jim's face and his reaction as he opens the magazine...

January 25, 2002

Well, Lord, yesterday was a high, but today was a low. The stupid, freaking computers have once again drained my strength. Sometimes life seems so totally hopeless without Jim. Now I have no e-mail (again) and You took away my beloved Troubleshooter. HOW am I going to get through the rest of my life without him? Help me out with this, please. I need a working computer desperately. This is REALLY bad timing, Lord.

January 26, 2002

WHAT IS GOING ON??? IS THIS SOME KIND OF TEST??? Mom broke her leg today — but then again, You already know that. I can't handle any more, Lord. Please help her. She is in so much pain, and I cannot stand to see her like that. Please give her relief, and please help her through the surgery tomorrow. And help ME to understand this nightmare.

January 27, 2002

Thank you for helping Mom through surgery. She still needs relief from pain. I can't bear to see her so uncomfortable. She is my strength, my rock; she holds ME up. I can't believe this is happening. How much do you think we can take? You have WAY too much confidence in me, Lord. And I have WAY too much on my plate...Mom, Anthony, work...and no Jim.

February 1, 2002

I am searching for answers to all of this madness — yet I find none. I really feel like we are being tested. If I didn't know any better, I'd swear someone put a curse on us. Anthony has a broken brain. Mom has a broken leg. And I have a broken heart. WHY?? WHY are you allowing us to suffer so much???

February 3, 2002
Went to church again today. Cried through the whole Mass. People were looking at me, and I didn't even care. Please give me strength, Lord, I really need it.

February 4, 2002
I read something today when I visited Mom at the rehab center. It said, "All pain can be a school in which one can learn." So, just what exactly are You trying to teach us, Lord?

February 5, 2002

Is your life aimed at something specific?

Well, it WAS...until Your plan and my plan butted heads. Now? I have no goals. My only mission is to get through each day. Please help me to do that. And every time you throw me a curve ball, help me not to get whiplash.

February 6, 2002

> *Our questions betray our lack of understanding: How can God be everywhere at one time? (Who says God is bound by a body?) How can God hear all the prayers which come to Him? (Perhaps His ears are different from yours.) How can God be the Father, the Son, and the Holy Spirit? (Could it be that Heaven has a different set of physics than earth?)*

141

These, and about 10,000 other questions I have for You, Lord. Like, WHY did you allow Jim's life to be taken and our happiness to be destroyed? And WHERE is Jim now? Can he see me? Can he hear me? How does this whole thing work? If he can see me, then he knows how unhappy and miserable I am, and then he'll be upset to see me this way...so certainly he can't be in Heaven if he's able to feel "sad." Is it true there's no negative emotions in Heaven? Why did You take him away from me?

February 8, 2002

> *Jesus knows how you feel. When you struggle, He listens. When you yearn, He responds. When you question, He hears. He has been there.*

Lord, You know how lost I feel without Jim. But if he can't be with me, then I suppose there's only one other person I would want him to be with: You.

February 11, 2002

Five months. Still can't believe it. I do not want to remember that day. I cannot imagine his last moments. Did Jim pray to you, Lord? Did he ask You for mercy? And if he was too scared to pray, did You give him a chance to talk to you before You judged him? Help me to control these thoughts, Lord. They are destroying me.

February 13, 2002

142

Today is Ash Wednesday. Sorry, but I'm not going to give up anything for Lent this year. I've decided that I've given up enough already.

February 14, 2002
I used to love Valentine's Day. Now I hate it. Dread it. Glad it's over, because if I saw one more sickening TV commercial for Zales jewelers or 1-800-FLOWERS, I was gonna throw something at the screen. Lord, You know where Jim is. And if You choose to, You can get a message to him: Please tell him I said, "Je t'aime beaucoup, all the days of my life…"

February 16, 2002
Lord, I think that if I knew for absolute sure that Jim was really enjoying his new life, I could be happy for him and it would be easier for me to move on with my own. But I still have so many questions…so much anxiety…so little understanding of how this whole afterlife thing works. My mind starts thinking about the worst case scenario, and I can't go down that road without having a meltdown. Where is he? Has he truly found ultimate peace and happiness? Will I see him again one day? Can you promise me this?

February 17, 2002
If I could ask You for just one more thing, ever again…if I only had one wish left…I would ask You to please let Jim be with You in heaven.

February 19, 2002

How does your prayer life today compare with a year or two ago?

143

Every single facet of my life is different now. But my prayer life has seen some significant changes. I always believed in You, Lord, but I never showed You the respect You deserve. I thought I was close to you before, but now I realize that I never really knew you. Back then, I was too "busy" for you. I never would have taken time out of my day to talk to you or write to you. Help me to get better at this. Help me to be more like You.

February 20, 2002
I remember a few months ago, my head was spinning with un-healthy thoughts...thoughts I did not know how to control...they were consuming me. I know I could not think clearly because I was spending all my energy being livid with You. I realize now that Willem and Ethel appeared in my life right around the height of my fury...and soon after, David Taylor gave me a big reason to smile...so there I was, cursing You out. And there You were, planting angels in my life when I wasn't looking. Thank you, Lord.

February 21, 2002

Describe the wonders you imagine are waiting for you in Heaven.

You are waiting there for me, Lord. And I imagine Jim is waiting there for me. What more could I ask for? One day, You will wel-come me into Your home and You'll answer all my questions. And I pray that one day, Jim and I will be reunited...together we will dive Galapagos and explore Saturn.

February 22, 2002

144

Think back over your life. How has Christ been changing you into his likeness?

Thinking back over my life — especially the past five months — is painful. And it's scary to look ahead to what appears to be an empty future. My heart is shattered, yet You assure me that You've got everything under control, as hard as that is for me to imagine right now. You are the driver, and I am the passenger in this thing called *life*.

February 23, 2002

> *God says that the more hopeless your circumstances, the more likely your salvation. The greater your cares, the more genuine your prayers. The darker the room, the greater the need for light. God's help is near and always available, but it is only given to those who seek it.*

Okay, I am seeking it, Lord. I can't do this without You. I still feel so hurt that the very happiness for which I prayed for so long was given to me, then taken away. But I must believe that You have Your reasons. Every day I read the Study Bible that Maria and Tom gave me, searching for answers. I must not be looking in the right places.

February 24, 2002

What is the purpose of setting your sights on God?

I realize now that I am only a pen in Your hand. You are the Author, the Creator of my biography, my life. If I run out of ink, You refill me. If I skip, You shake me up a bit, so I write smoothly again. If I roll off the desk, You pick me up and guide me back to the page. Thanks for all that.

145

March 2, 2002

> *You want to make a difference in your world? Live*
> *a holy life: Be faithful to your spouse. Be the one*
> *at the office who refuses to cheat. Be the neighbor*
> *who acts neighborly. Be the employee who does the*
> *work and doesn't complain. Pay your bills. Do*
> *your part and enjoy life. Don't speak one message*
> *and live another.*

Okay, I have done all of that plus more. But You never promised
that "living a holy life" would protect us from pain and suffering,
right? Guess I'm the poster child for that. But You did promise
us that you wouldn't abandon us, that you'd be there with us
through our darkest hours. Even though it sure seemed like You
deserted me five months ago, I am beginning to see that You did
not desert me at all.

March 5, 2002
Bad day. That envelope from the Medical Examiner got me all
worked up. Had to take a Xanax for the first time in a long time.
This is a delicate subject and You know how sensitive I am about
it. You know how I feel — my fears, my wishes. Please just
search my soul because I can't write about it. Help me through
this, Lord.

March 8, 2002

> *The true children of God are those who let God's*
> *Spirit lead them."*
>
> ~ Romans 8:14

From what I've been reading, I am supposed to control only the things that I can and leave the rest up to you. Well, You know what a control freak I am, Lord. It's so hard to relinquish it. Yet I am finding, only recently, that I really do feel...calmer...when I just hand You the wheel. Help me to continue this.

March 9, 2002

> *God is not the God of confusion, and wherever He sees sincere seekers with confused hearts, you can bet your sweet December that He will do whatever it takes to help them see His will.*

Got incredible news from Elke today! Apparently she broke through the island's political red tape and got permission for the plaque she's been talking about. I'm trying not to get my hopes up, Lord, I don't want to be disappointed. I know how easily these things can fall through. But...if there's any way You can make this happen...what an amazing dedication to Jim...if this be your will.

March 11, 2002

If someone told me one year ago today that I'd be losing someone I love in six months, I would have automatically assumed it would be Anthony because of his brain tumor. I never could have imagined it would be Jim. I thank you for letting us keep Anthony. I wish you had let me keep Jim, too.

March 17, 2002

> *Consider the price of Christ's gift. Think of what it cost Him to come to earth and die for our salvation.*

I guess You know all about pain. I guess You can identify with suffering. And the more I dwell in despair about mine, the more I minimize Yours. How can I ever express my gratitude for Your sacrifice? There are not enough words. You will have to look inside my heart.

March 20, 2002
Well, this wasn't one of my better days. I was impatient and short-tempered with people at work...I snapped at Mom a few times on the phone...I'm really having a hard time accepting this new life I didn't ask for. Inexcusable behavior, though. Please help me to be better tomorrow, Lord.

March 24, 2002
Easter is getting close now. I think about it more and more, and I realize now that I never acknowledged this holiday with the sincerity that I should have. But it's much more important to me now, since I'm faced with the reality of Jim's eternity, and one day, my own.

March 25, 2002

> *God has kept no secrets. He has told us that, while on this yellow brick road of life, we will experience trouble. Disease will afflict bodies. Divorce will break hearts. Death will make widows and devastation will destroy countries. We should not expect any less...but we needn't panic. The battle is over. The manuscript has been published. The book has been bound...*

148

Lord, I need You in my life. I'm not panicking, but I need You to rescue me from my loneliness. Without Jim, I feel so alone, so unhappy. Help me to do something with my life that stops me from dwelling on my loss...something that makes me happy again, something that allows me to smile instead of cry when I think of Jim.

March 29, 2002
Today is Good Friday. I now have a whole new respect and appreciation for what You did for us. You gave us the greatest gift imaginable: the opportunity to live forever. You do so much for us...yet You ask so little of us...and we give You so little in return.

March 30, 2002

> *God has an incredible plan for your life. Write about how you see His plan unfolding for your good and His glory.*

I see You using me to help others through difficult times. Certainly not right away, for I am not yet strong enough. But this whole thing is a true test of patience. I read something today from St. Augustine: "Faith sometimes falters, because God does not reward us immediately. But hold out, be steadfast, bear the delay, and you have carried the cross." I know I have to be patient. You do not always work quickly. Heck, it took You thirty-one years to hook me up with Jim.

March 31, 2002 — Easter Sunday
I can honestly say that this has been my best day since 9/11, because of what day it is and what it now means to me. Because of Your own resurrection, You opened the door for us, and You

149

hold it open and welcome us in. Thank You for everything you have done for me, and everything You continue to do.

April 1, 2002

> *The cross was no accident. Jesus' death wasn't a tragic surprise...It was part of an incredible plan. It was a calculated choice.*

Was 9/11 one of Your calculated choices, Lord? Or a tragic surprise? I struggle with this, because it's still so hard for me to accept that You would plan it — or allow it.

April 2, 2002

Today was a rough day — my birthday — but thanks to my family, I got through it. I would have preferred to stay in bed all day, but Mom and Maria wouldn't hear of it. They kidnapped me and took me out to lunch and treated me to a pedicure. I am realizing that my family is beyond "family." They are icons of Your power. You provide strength to me *through* them.

April 3, 2002

I met with sculptor Brian Hanlon today; I told him about the urgency for getting Jim's Cayman plaque done ASAP. He was so understanding and willing to do whatever it takes. Lord, I think You have put another angel in my life. Thank You.

April 5, 2002

150

Lord, You are the only one who can bring me peace and comfort, either directly or through other people. And You are the only one who can give me the answers I so desperately need...You are the only one who can assure me that I will indeed see Jim again. I need You in my life.

April 9, 2002

> *It wasn't right that spikes pierced the hands that formed the earth. And it wasn't right that the Son of God was forced to hear the silence of God. It wasn't right, but it happened. For while Jesus was on the cross, God sat on His hands. He turned His back. He ignored the screams of the innocent. He sat in silence while the sins of the world were placed upon His Son. And He did nothing while a cry a million times bloodier than John's echoed in the black sky: 'My God, My God, why have you forsaken me?' ...Was it right? No. Was it fair? No. Was it love? Yes.*

I think I know how Jesus must have felt. I felt the same way on 9/11. How I cursed at you, screamed at you, so furious with you. So full of anger and hostility and hurt and bitterness. I remember those days, and I am ashamed. I'm still not seeing the reason for all of this, but I believe someday you will reveal it to me.

April 10, 2002

> *I can't understand it. I honestly cannot. Why did Jesus die on the cross? Could it be that His heart was broken for all the people who cast despairing eyes toward the dark heavens and cry the same 'WHY?' Could it be that His heart was broken for the hurting? ...I picture His eyes misting and a*

151

pierced hand brushing away a tear...He who also
was once alone, understands.

I suppose You do understand, more than anyone possibly could, the grief I live with. And it has become clear to me that You have indeed brushed away my tears...You have sent angels into my life to help me through my darkest moments. You really do understand. Now please help me accept this.

April 11, 2002
On the way to work today, there was an awful car accident by the light. Then there was a fire behind the pharmacy, and someone lost their home. Several people's lives were changed dramatically today. I know how that feels. I found out first-hand, seven months ago today. Lord, please help them through difficult times ahead.

April 13, 2002
Lord, please bless and reward all the people who put together the VFW dinner dance today and all those who donated so generously to the 9/11 families. It was an emotionally exhausting night, very difficult. Thanks for giving me the strength to get up in front of 300 people to accept that beautiful Bible in Jim's memory.

April 24, 2002
Today at work someone brought in a parable about how birds got their wings. They started out wingless...then You, God, put the wings down in front of them and told them to fly. At first, they couldn't because they were weighted down with the burden of the heavy wings at their feet. But they eventually learned to lay them on their shoulders and carry them. Then they soared.

Please help me to carry this burden, Lord. Please teach me how to fly. I'm scared...

152

April 27, 2002
I can't believe I painted the downstairs bathroom all by myself. Tore down the wallpaper, spackled, sanded, primed, and painted it "sunshine yellow." I doubt Jim would have approved of the color. Tomorrow I'll stripe it with semigloss...might need Your help with that. You're a fairly decent artist. Look at what You do with sunsets.

April 29, 2002
The window of opportunity for getting the plaque finished, shipped to Cayman, and mounted by June 1 is getting smaller and smaller. I'm really trying not to get upset. I've been trying to follow Ethel's advice and "cast my anxieties upon You"...but maybe this whole thing was just not meant to be. If that's the case, please help me accept it. For that matter, help me accept the whole reason WHY we're memorializing Jim in the first place.

May 1, 2002
I dread this whole month. Two anniversaries and Jim's birthday. All I can do is take a deep breath, jump in, swim through the month until I reach June, then come up for air. I will need Your help, Lord. You're much more effective than Xanax.

May 3, 2002
Tomorrow is a day I've been dreading. Our wedding anniversary. It was the happiest day of our lives, and I hate that now the mere thought of it turns a knot in my stomach. I hate that the very day which once made me smile more than any other, now makes me cry. I cried all night tonight, just thinking about tomorrow. My brother Anthony just quietly held me on the sofa while I sobbed...he didn't say anything. He knew there wasn't anything he could possibly say.

153

I thank You for giving me the most special brother anyone could ask for. And I ask You to be with me tomorrow. I will need You, desperately.

May 4, 2002
I told my family and friends that I needed to be alone today. They granted my wish. Actually, I'm hoping I wasn't really alone. I'm hoping Jim was sitting next to me as I watched every one of our home movies, including our wedding video. After all, this was OUR day, and we always did something special. How I miss him. What I wouldn't do to see him again...just for 30 seconds...just to tell him one more time, how much I love him.

Lord, please tell Jim — in case he doesn't already know this — that I say my wedding vows to him every single night before I go to bed...and I always will.

And I thank You, Lord, for giving me the happiest six years of my life, with Jim.

May 8, 2002
Today I received a thank you note from a woman who lost her husband on the *Wave Dancer*. Lord, help her to be strong and to endure this new life that we're both stuck with. She lost Ray exactly seven months ago today.

May 11, 2002
Eight months without him. Today I saw a bookmark in Barnes and Noble...it said: "Teach me to let go of yesterday, live fully today, and look with excitement toward tomorrow."

Easier said than done.

May 13, 2002
Brian finished the plaque today. I'm FedExing it to Cayman to-

morrow...then it will be totally out of my control, and You know how that concept unnerves me. So I ask You, Lord...please help me accept whatever comes — or doesn't come — of this.

May 20, 2002
Tonight I read Romans 12, and I realized that there are many gifts You have given me, and I do not appreciate them or even thank You for them. The knowledge of pharmacy and meds is a gift, yet I complain about my profession and treat it like it was meaningless. How must that make You feel? How would I feel if I gave someone a gift and they threw it away?

May 24, 2002
Tough day. Today is Jim's thirty-ninth birthday. Did he jinx himself by joking about how he wasn't gonna make it to the age of forty? I can still hear his voice in my mind, all the time. I talk to him, and I wonder if he can hear me. I pray, Lord, that he's having his best birthday ever.

May 27, 2002
Today was the last hurdle for this most difficult month. I can't believe it was seven years ago today that Jim and I met. I wonder what Your plans are...how long before we meet again? Please tell him that I left a rose for him outside our "table" where we met at TGI Friday's.

May 28, 2002
Today I opened Elke's e-mail and couldn't believe my eyes...the plaque is underwater! I am so grateful to her, to everyone in Cayman, and to You, Lord...for making this happen. My heart is bursting with pride for Jim...thank You, thank You, Lord.

Right after I read Elke's big news, I got an e-mail from Ethel.

She knows nothing about the plaque yet...but ironically, she quoted Matthew 21:21-22 (NASB) and I don't think there's a more appropriate verse for the occasion:

> And Jesus answered and said to them, "Truly I say to you, if you have faith and do not doubt, you will not only do what was done to the fig tree, but even if you say to this mountain, 'Be taken up and cast into the sea,' it will happen. 'And all things you ask in prayer, believing, you will receive."

June 7, 2002

> God never said that the journey would be easy, but he did say that the arrival would be worthwhile.

I pray that Jim has arrived in a place where he is SO happy that he would never want to come back here if he were given the choice. Not even for me.

June 10, 2002

> Don't ask God to do what you want. Ask Him to do what is right.

I guess this was the big *faux pas* of my prayers, right, Lord? All my life, I always prayed for what I wanted. Me, me, me. Never thought for a minute that You had MY best interest in mind. Always assumed I knew the best course of action — all I needed You for was to make it all happen. Too bad it took such an enormous tragedy in my life to realize my mistake...

156

A 9/11 Diary

June 12, 2002

> *Healthy marriages have a sense of 'remaining.'*
> *The husband remains in the wife, and she re-*
> *mains in him. There is a tenderness, an honesty,*
> *an ongoing communication. The same is true in*
> *our relationship with God...People who live long*
> *lives together eventually begin to sound alike, to*
> *talk alike, even to think alike. As we walk with*
> *God, we take on His thoughts, His principles, His*
> *attitudes. We take on His heart.*

Okay, so maybe Jim and I didn't have a "long" life together. Certainly not long enough. But I believe in soul mates, and I'm certain he is mine. It took me a long time after 9/11 to be able to say Jim's name or talk about him without bursting into tears. Now, Lord, I want to recall our memories with joy instead of sadness. Help me to do that, because it still doesn't come easily. As far as You and I are concerned...we weren't on the same wavelength for a while. But You waited patiently for me to come around, and now I must do the same. I must wait patiently for You to bring me peace...and maybe even some happiness.

June 14, 2002

> *We need to hear that God is still in control. We*
> *need to hear that it's not over until He says so. We*
> *need to hear that life's mishaps and tragedies are*
> *not a reason to bail out. They are simply a reason*
> *to sit tight.*

I never thought I would say this, but...surrendering control of my life to You has really reduced my stress level. I'm not imagining it; I'm sure of it. You are a "Cure for disappointment," Lord.

June 17, 2002

> *Yesterday you cannot alter, but your reaction to yesterday you can. The past you cannot change, but your response to your past you can. Think about how anger makes life miserable...*

I think back to how I boycotted You during those first few months. I was so angry; You appeared to have let me down hard — by not answering my prayers the way I wanted and expected You to. But You cleverly positioned my family, my friends, and even a few strangers in my life to help lessen that anger. Thank You, Lord, for Your intervention in my life.

June 19, 2002
If I was as close to you on 9/11 as I am now, would I still have reacted with such anger? Would I have sensed Your presence in spite of the circumstances? If I trusted You with my life then (which I didn't) as I do now, would my "recovery" have been that much easier? Would I have had the ability to recognize why I only saw *one* set of footprints?

June 22, 2002

> *God's lights in our dark nights are as numerous as the stars, if only we'll look for them.*

158

Nine months ago, I was searching for a blinding floodlight, and I didn't see one, so I sat in darkness. By choice, of course. Took me a while to realize that light doesn't necessarily come from one single source. When I finally woke up and looked around, I saw that You had given me quite a few 40-watt bulbs. Thanks for that, Lord.

June 28, 2002
Lord, today I recalled a conversation that Jim and I had years ago...although he was a life-long Catholic, Jim wanted to visit a different denomination. I flipped out at his suggestion. I was stubborn and close-minded...of course, he dropped the subject and that was the end of that. But now I feel so guilty about it. He wanted something more. He wanted to expand his spiritual limits, and I cut him down. Please, Lord, tell him I'm so sorry.

July 1, 2002
Today, Eileen and I talked about my anxiety over the Cayman trip. I told her, "This is not a vacation. It's going to be like a funeral." She said, "Only if you make it that way."

July 5, 2002

> *Bitterness is its own poison. The dungeon, deep and dark, is beckoning you to enter. You can, you know. You've experienced enough hurt...You can choose, like many, to chain yourself to hurt...Or you can choose, like some, to put away your hurts before they become hates. How does God deal with your bitter heart? He reminds you that what you have is more important than what you don't have. You still have your relationship with God. No one can take that.*

159

Wow, this hits the nail on the head. I did have that choice, and I'm glad I made the right decision. Please help me to focus on the things that I do still have...there are so many people and things in my life that I would miss so dearly if they were taken from me...my family, my friends, my health, my freedom, my home, my memories...Thank You, Lord, for all of these, and everything You give to me.

July 7, 2002

I'm really having a hard time concentrating at work. I keep thinking about Jim, about Cayman and the plaque, about the whole trip. I keep thinking about this time last year, as Jim and I renovated the family room, so certain of our plans. Can't believe I'll be returning to Cayman next week. Not with Jim, but FOR Jim.

July 10, 2002

Now I'm thinking back to this day in 2000, when Anthony was diagnosed with terminal brain cancer. You really do put bizarre twists in our lives, don't You?

July 13, 2002

You know I can be somewhat clueless, Lord, when it comes to recognizing Your intervention in my life. I fear that I might mistake my own desires with what I believed to be Your intentions. Tomorrow we leave for Cayman, and I pray to You that everything goes smoothly...I must keep reminding myself that You're the one running the show.

July 14, 2002

We are in Grand Cayman, and it's been quite an emotional day for me, seeing all the familiar faces and places. Help me to show

Maria and Tom why we loved this island so much. Please, Lord, get me through this week.

July 15, 2002

Elke and I were talking about Jim today, and she said, "He spoiled us with his presence. And I don't mean all those presents he gave us." I second the motion. Thank You, Lord, for giving us all the opportunity to know and love Jim. His very existence changed our lives.

July 16, 2002

I pray for us to have good weather and good health tomorrow, Lord, for the memorial dive. I can't imagine that you would take us this far and involve so many people and not let this go smoothly. But You're full of surprises, so I must be prepared for a curve ball. I am so nervous about this dive tomorrow, Lord. Anxiety and diving don't mix. Please help me through this.

July 17, 2002

How do I even begin to thank You for today? You made it so obvious to us that Jim is okay, that he's happy, that he knows what we've done for him, and that he is so proud of it! It felt like a slice of heaven down there today. All my anxiety just disappeared, and in its place came peace. It could not have been more perfect. I cannot express my feelings with words. Please just know, Lord, how much I love You.

July 20, 2002

Before we left Cayman today, I thanked Elke for all she had done. She said, "I only thought of the idea. There is a Higher One who brought it all together and made it happen." Thank You, Higher One. And thanks for a safe flight home.

July 28, 2002

I still feel a strong sense of renewal. Is it my imagination? Am I still on a high from the memorial dive? I think back to how I felt 317 days ago and in the months that followed. I compare today with how I felt back then. I never dreamt that I could find any peace in my life again. But I never prayed for peace in those days. I didn't pray at all. I have never felt Your presence in my life more than I did last week. "Believe the unbelievable. Receive the inconceivable."

August 3, 2002

I realize, Lord, that my situation could be much more tragic than it is. Like, what if something tragic had happened to Jim while we were diving? What if I couldn't save him and he died in my arms, under water? That's an image I would never have been able to live with. Seeing towers collapse in my mind is bad enough...but if I saw Jim's face as he took his last breath — I know I couldn't handle it. And I would have been alone on an island, no family around. And I wouldn't have gotten the generous donations that allowed me to take time off from work. And there NEVER would have been a spread in a magazine with Jim's photos...and there NEVER would have been a dive site and memorial plaque. My life would be so much different. So much...worse.

August 5, 2002

> *When we submit to God's plans, we can trust our desires. Our assignment is found at the intersection of God's plan and our pleasures.*

162

I yield myself entirely to You, Lord. I trust You to guide and direct my life. Sometimes I don't trust myself to recognize Your cues, so I might need some help with that. Help me to always find that intersection where You and I meet.

August 11, 2002

Eleven months ago, I had no hope of finding peace, no hope of smiling again, no hope of even functioning again. I never thought I would make it this far. People tell me that I am strong. I tell them, "I don't feel strong. But if I am, it's because of my family, my friends, and my faith." Gotta give credit where credit is due. Thank You, Lord.

August 13, 2002

Mrs. Brocco's husband John died yesterday. You know she has been like a grandmother to me, Lord. She has been so kind to me, and now I must be there for her. Today at the funeral Mass, she actually mentioned Jim in the eulogy. Even in her most difficult moments, she's still thinking about other people. Help me to be more like her, Lord.

August 17, 2002

> *God's delight is received upon surrender, not awarded upon conquest...Those who taste God's presence have declared spiritual bankruptcy and are aware of their spiritual crisis...Their pockets are empty. Their options are gone. They have long since stopped demanding justice; they are pleading for mercy.*

163

Before 9/11, I'd say my spiritual pockets were only half-full. On that day and for a few months after, they were inside out and some loose change fell out. I hit rock bottom and I was virtually bankrupt. But there was enough loose change to make a desperate phone call — to You, Lord — and You sent help in the form of a tremendous support group of family, friends, neighbors, and complete strangers. Thank You, Lord, for paying me back with interest.

August 20, 2002

Everyone is talking about what they're doing for the 9/11 anniversary. I try so hard not to think about it. I dread it, fiercely. But it is inevitable, and I ask You to help me confront it when the time comes. I will need Your strength, Lord.

August 25, 2002

Seven years ago today, Jim asked me to marry him, and I didn't think it was possible to be any happier than I was at that moment. But each day with him, I loved him deeper and deeper. One year ago today, we were in New York with Mom and Dad to see *Phantom of the Opera* (for the fifth time) and to have dinner at Four Seasons. Never could I have imagined where I would be today: placing a rose on the "Grieving Angel" next to Jim's name and picture. Lord, please tell him I said, "Happy Engagement Anniversary, hon!"

August 28, 2002

> *We must trust God. We must trust not only that He does what is best but that He knows what is ahead. Ponder the words of Isaiah 57:1-2 (TLB): 'The good men perish; the godly die before their time and no one seems to care or wonder why. No one seems to realize that God is taking them away*

from the evil days ahead. For the godly who die shall rest in peace."

I trust that you took Jim for a good reason. Perhaps his job here was finished. (It's still hard to swallow that one.) Perhaps You needed him elsewhere. (If there are computers in heaven, I bet he's writing code for You.) Or maybe You...rescued him.

August 29, 2002
I believe You have some kind of a plan for me, Lord. So I will lie still in Your arms, patiently waiting and trusting You. In case You haven't noticed, I've stopped asking "WHY?" I trust that You will give me those answers when we finally meet. I look forward to that day. And I so look forward to meeting You, Lord.

September 4, 2002
I am terrified of next week, Lord. I know You want us to cast our fears and anxieties onto you...but then I wonder: Why did You create the emotions of fear and worry and anxiety in the first place?

September 9, 2002
Time is closing in on the day I dread. Please keep me calm, Lord. Again I find myself thinking back to what Jim and I did one year ago. We spent the day together on the new bike trail then went out to dinner with Cindy and Johnny. Two days later, our lives changed forever. Please God, give me strength to get through this.

September 10, 2002
I am in New York at the Wall Street Regent with Mom and Maria in my room. I am terrified of tomorrow, Lord. I can't see Ground Zero from where I am now. I don't want to go there, but

I feel like I owe it to Jim to be here. I already feel sick to my stomach. For the past year, I have survived on avoiding the images of that day. Tomorrow I will confront it head on. Please God, help me through it. Please be with me.

September 11, 2002

I have never been so happy to be home. I am emotionally and physically spent, Lord. I know that some — many? — people find peace at Ground Zero. I for one did not. It was an ugly, raw, devastating pit and a reminder of a day I don't want to remember. Unlike Cayman, I did not return with a sense that Jim was there. Why would he go back there? I certainly won't be returning. The wind was spooky; people were insisting it was the "spirits of the victims." Thank you for getting me through it. Now help me to move on.

September 12, 2002

The seed buried in the earth will blossom in heaven. Your soul and body will reunite, and you will be like Jesus...Death is not a time for us to despair, but a time to trust.

When I think of how I feel today, compared with this day last year, I shudder. I am two completely different people. I am so sorry, Lord, for my anger with you back then ... my violent temper, my profanity directed at you, my bitterness and fury. I know you expected me to feel that way. Thank you for never leaving me, even when I thought you had.

A 9/11 Diary

September 14, 2002

> *Oh, the power of our hands. Leave them unman-*
> *aged and they become weapons: clawing for power,*
> *strangling for survival, seducing for pleasure. But*
> *manage them and our hands become instruments of*
> *grace — not just tools in the hands of God, but*
> *God's very hands...How does God use your hands?*

Makes me realize yet another thing I take for granted, Lord. Just as I couldn't imagine my life without Jim, I cannot fathom my life without the use of my hands. I would not be able to work as a pharmacist. I would not be able to write e-mails to my friends every night. I would not be able to play the piano. I would not be able to cook and bake and do so many things that I enjoy doing. And...I would not be able to write to You every night. Now *that* would be a tragedy.

September 15, 2002

It seems a bit easier now, to look ahead. The first year without Jim is over. I already know how it feels to be without him; I already know what to expect. Not that life will be easy — far from it. But with You in my life, I believe I can get through anything.

September 27, 2002

> *"Surely I spoke of things I did not understand; I*
> *talked of things too wonderful for me to know.' (Job*
> *42:3) God is God. He knows what He is doing.*
> *When you can't trace His hand, trust His heart."*

167

I think every one of us can relate to Job in some way. Okay, maybe we didn't lose as much as he did — at least not all at once — but we feel his pain, and we admire his endurance, and I'm inspired by his faith. And like Job, I asked You a thousand times, "why?" ...but I had to settle for just one answer: You know what you're doing.

September 30, 2002

Lord, I snapped at a few people at work today. I had one nerve left, and they got on it. I am sorry for reacting that way, and I told them so. But it's still so hard to keep my focus on this job... sometimes I wonder if I should continue doing this. Lord, give me something to do with my life. Something else. Either in addition to pharmacy, or instead of it...something that would please You. Maybe something that would help others the way so many people helped me...

October 3, 2002

I have changed so much in the past year, Lord. But I've still got a long way to go. Please help me to expand my limits — all of them — my physical, mental, emotional, and spiritual limits; my limits of patience, understanding, and wisdom; my limits of generosity, compassion, and kindness; even my limits of faith and trust in You.

October 6, 2002

Lord, please be with Anthony — he had a seizure today, first one in over a year. He needs You. We all need You.

October 8, 2002

You are a great God...Your truth is absolute...Your strength is unending...Your provisions are abundant for our needs...Your plan is perfect. Bewildering. Puzzling. Troubling. But perfect.

Lord, please be with Teresa today...it was one year ago that Ray died, and I know how hard this day will be for her. Remind us both that one day we will understand how these tragedies fit into Your magnificent, perfect plan.

October 10, 2002

It has come to my attention that You actually want us to RE-JOICE IN our suffering, not simply accept them. ("For suffering produces perseverance; and perseverance, character; and character, hope; and hope does not disappoint...") I suppose our trials do make us stronger and wiser. And if that's the case, I should soon be competition for Hercules and Confucius.

October 13, 2002

Why do we always tend to choose the side of safety? What can you do to step out into God's adventure for your life?

I am not reckless, but I'm not afraid to take certain chances that I once never would have done. I have absolutely no fear of death, Lord. In fact, I look forward to it. (No, this is not a suicide note.) I can't wait to finally see You and to be with Jim again. I have committed myself to live my life according to Your Word, Your will, Your love, and my faith in You. I trust You, Lord. Work Your will through me.

October 16, 2002

> *The purpose of the Bible is to proclaim God's plan and passion to save His children. That is the reason this book has endured through the centuries... It is the treasure map that leads us to God's highest treasure: eternal life.*

I can't say I've found the answers I'm looking for in there, Lord, but I've certainly found comfort and peace for my soul.

October 22, 2002

> *There is a window in your heart through which you can see God. Once upon a time that window was clear...then suddenly, the window cracked. A pebble broke the window. A pebble of pain. You were puzzled. God wouldn't allow something like this to happen, would he? When you can't see Him, trust Him...Jesus is closer than you've ever dreamed.*

I can still hear myself saying this to You. "You wouldn't let this happen, would You? I prayed to you this morning to bring him home safely!!!"

I trust that You have done that. I'm sorry that I ever doubted You. When we finally meet, are You going to say, "See, I told you!"?

170 October 26, 2002

Today I spent a long time visiting the "Angel." Brought a flower (silk this time) to put on Jim's ledge. It was quiet there, no one around because it's too cold. I am captivated by her expression. She feels what I feel.

October 28, 2002

The days are getting shorter now, and the nights longer. Today is Day 413. I think back to this time last year. I had just gotten his death certificate. His car got towed away. I was swallowing Xanax by the handful. I was a mess. Thank You, Lord, for steering me to a better life.

November 2, 2002

Went to the dentist today. He told me I must be clenching my teeth when I sleep (don't doubt it), and its creating havoc. After all those years of braces and straight teeth, they're going crooked again. Oh, but this should be the least of my problems. I won't ask You to keep my teeth straight, Lord. But I will ask You to keep my path straight.

November 3, 2002

> *Sometimes God is speaking but we do not hear him. Sometimes he is answering our prayer but we think he has done nothing.*

Sounds familiar, wouldn't You say, Lord? One thing I have learned is that You answer our prayers creatively, and according to Your will, not necessarily our wishes. Makes me think twice before I select my words to You. ("Be careful what you wish for...")

171

November 8, 2002

> *Jesus was able to bear shame on earth knowing*

what awaited Him in heaven. Do you know what awaits you in heaven?

I imagine heaven this way: First, I see You. You welcome me with a warm, gripping embrace filled with love that I finally compre-hend. I am so excited to actually see You and be with You, I can hardly contain myself. You promise me that all of my questions will be answered..."but first, there is someone who's been waiting to see you..." And You step aside as Jim comes forward and I see his beaming smile. And my eternity is complete.

November 13, 2002

Worship is the 'thank you' that refuses to be si-lenced. Worship is a voluntary act of gratitude of-fered by the saved to the Savior, by the healed to the Healer, and by the delivered to the Deliverer.

Thank You, Lord, for rescuing me. You are my Hero. Thank You for healing me. You are my personal Physician. Thank You for advising me. You are my spiritual Attorney. Thank You for calm-ing me. You are my mental health Coordinator. Thank You for renovating me. You are quite the Architect.

November 22, 2002

There are times when the one thing you want is the one thing you will never get...What if God says no? ...Content. That's the word. A state of heart in which you would be at peace if God gave you nothing more than he already has.

I think I could be in the "content" stage if we add a clause to that: If You gave me nothing more than I already have — AND if you did not take away anything or anyone else in my life — then I shall be content with my current circumstances. I'm not saying I like it. I've just learned to live with it and make the best of it.

November 28, 2002 — Thanksgiving
Last year, I was in such a state of turmoil, I felt I had nothing to be thankful for. My gift had been taken away from me. This year, I realize I have so much to be thankful for. I have the greatest family and friends that anyone could want. And I've made my peace with You, Lord. And I give my thanks to You.

November 29, 2002

> *Only you can surrender your concerns to the Father. Only you can cast all your anxieties on the one who cares for you.*

It's true, I admit it, I have not yet mastered the art of surrendering my concerns to you. I still carry the weight on my back, and sometimes my knees buckle from the heavy load. I ask You to "remove my anxiety," but there's my mistake: I need to cast them onto You. It's my part that requires the action. I must drop the load at Your feet instead of asking You to take it off my back. I shall try harder, Lord.

December 4, 2002
I've decided not to put up a Christmas tree again this year. There are certain things that I'm still not strong enough to do, and that's one of them. Maybe next year. Instead, I bought a Nativity

set. Never had one before. It's remarkably beautiful. Makes me feel much closer to You than a lighted spruce in my living room.

December 12, 2002
As much as I try to avoid it, I am falling into the fast pace of the Christmas season. I resist, but the rest of the world is pulling me along. I hate the commercialism. It does not honor You. On the contrary, it minimizes and suffocates You. Who started this whole production of trees and stockings and presents? I don't mean to sound like Scrooge, but I think You deserve so much...less.

December 20, 2002
Spent a few minutes with the "Angel" today. Cried a bit. I guess I still have some reality bricks that hit me, like today. I get that feeling in the pit of my stomach when I think about waking up Christmas morning without Jim. Yes, life is easier than it was last year...but it ain't easy.

December 23, 2002
Bad day today. Meltdown at work. I just couldn't seem to control it; I was overpowered by emotions and happy people all around me who have spouses to go home to. Got home and fell apart again. Please help me, Lord, to concentrate on what I have, instead of what I have lost. I love You, Lord.

December 24, 2002
The only gifts I have that are worthy of giving to you tomorrow: undying love, unbroken allegiance, ceaseless praise. Please help me get through tomorrow, Lord. I love You.

174

December 25, 2002
You were born to this earth to save us. And what a difficult, frus-

trating life You led. What pain, suffering, and persecution You endured for us. When You were told who You were (at age 12?) You did not doubt it or resist it. You accepted it. Help me to be like You, Lord, to accept whatever is — or is not — ahead for me. Happy Birthday, Jesus. I love You.

December 31, 2002
I thank You for this past year, Lord, and for getting me through every day without Jim. I thank You for my incredible family, who continues to be my strongest support. I thank You for giving Mom strength to recover from her broken leg and for giving Anthony endurance to sustain his many trials.

I thank You for the amazing tributes to Jim...I thank You for all the new friendships I have made this year...proof that sometimes good things arise from bad situations. I thank You for the countless longtime friends that have been with me from the very beginning of this journey...I trust that You will bless every one of them for their kindness to me.

I will never forget what You have given me and done for me. I will also never forget the one You took from me.

Help me through this next year, Lord. And remind me that nothing is going to happen to me that You and I together can't handle.

tf

Helps &
Resources

No matter who you are, or whom you have lost, you are never alone in your grief. In addition to the "crutches" I acknowledge in the book — my family, my friends, and my faith — I wish to share some special resources that helped me through my darkest hours. I hope you will also find comfort and support in them.

Literature
A Grief Observed, C.S.Lewis

Chicken Soup for the Grieving Soul: Stories About Life, Death, and Overcoming the Loss of a Loved One, Jack Canfield, Mark Victor Hansen

I Wasn't Ready To Say Goodbye: Surviving, Coping, and Healing After the Sudden Death of a Loved One, Brook Noel, Pamela Blair

On Death And Dying, Elizabeth Kubler-Ross

The Courage To Grieve, Judy Tatelbaum

Tuesdays With Morrie, Mitch Albom

When There Are No Words, Charlie Walton

God in My Grief, Thomas J. David

When Tragedy Strikes, Charles Stanley

Finding Your Way after Your Spouse Dies, Marta Felber

Websites
www.griefnet.org — (online support group)

www.griefshare.org — (Christian organization, helps people locate local support groups)

www.widownet.org — (self-help resource for and by widows)

www.groww.org — (Grief Recovery Online for Widows and Widowers)

Organizations
THEOS (They Help Each Other Spiritually)
Pittsburgh, PA — contact them for a group near you
412-471-7779

To Live Again
Springfield, PA
610-353-7740

Resources & Helps

Parents Without Partners
561-391-8833
www.parentswithoutpartners.org

Catholic Charities USA
703-549-1390
www.catholiccharitiesusa.org

MISSING

JAMES ("JIM") SANDS
Cantor Fitzgerald (eSpeed)
103rd Floor, Tower One